CELTIC BARDS, CELTIC DRUIDS

CELTIC BARDS, CELTIC DRUIDS

R.J. Stewart and Robin Williamson

Colour illustrations by Chris Down

BLANDFORD

First published in the UK 1996 by Blandford
A Cassell Imprint
CASSELL PLC
Wellington House
125 Strand
London WC2R 0BB

First published in paperback 1999

Distributed in the United States by Sterling Publishing
Co., Inc.
387 Park Avenue South, New York, NY 10016-8810

**A Cataloguing-in-Publication Data entry for this title is
available from the British Library**

ISBN 0-7137-2784-5

Colour illustrations, Celtic borders and motifs by
Chris Down
Black and white illustrations by Sarah Lever
Typeset by Keystroke, Jacaranda Lodge, Wolverhampton
Printed and bound in Spain.

In memory of Roberta Gray, who taught me about the
magical content of *The Mabinogion*, the bardic wisdom of
Iolo Morganwg, the myth of the 'Two Brothers' and
other Celtic sources of wisdom, between 1969 and 1973.

R. J. Stewart

And in memory of Ewan MacColl, the great bard and
ballad singer of the twentieth century.

R. J. Stewart and Robin Williamson

Grant, O Divine Being, thy Protection
And in Protection, Strength
And in Strength, Understanding
And in Understanding, Knowledge
And in Knowledge, the Knowledge of Justice
And in the Knowledge of Justice, the Love of Justice
And in that Love, the Love of all Beings
And in the Love of all Beings, the Love of Divine Being.

Translation from Welsh by R. J. Stewart of
'Druid Invocation at the Thirteen Stones'
which is recited by bards at the Gorsedd of Wales

CONTENTS

Part Three: Return to the Source –
Wisdom Through Inspiration – The
Light Within

ACKNOWLEDGEMENTS

We would like to acknowledge Josephine Stewart and Bina Williamson our wives, for their love, support and encouragement. Specifically Robin wishes to acknowledge Chris Hamlett for the use of his library of classical authors, Jan Krieshan for typing, and Dale and Lizzie for access to the 'Iolo' manuscript.

We would also like to acknowledge Derek Bryce for his good work at Llanerch Press, publishing valuable books on, and directly from, the Welsh and Celtic tradition. More specifically, it was his translation of Breton folk-tales that in 1989 drew our attention to the work of F. M. Luzel in the previous century and inspired us to work with these remarkable stories. Some of the Llanerch titles are listed in our Bibliography.

Thanks also to Chris Down for his excellent colour plates and to Sarah Lever for the black and white illustrations.

Some of the translations, poems and tales in this collection have appeared in earlier books of ours which are now out of print; they have been rewritten especially for this book.

R. J. S.
R. W.

PREFACE

e, the authors, have been friends for some years. We come from the same country, Scotland, and the same city, Edinburgh – and yet we both have strong Welsh connections. Inspired by Celtic tradition as performers, as musicians and as writers, it seemed inevitable – creatively – that we should come together on the theme of bards and druids.

Our aim has been to inspire, to inform and to show how, from the earliest to the most recent sources, the roots of Celtic tradition still manifest themselves in many forms in the imagination. The oldest forms are those ancestral traditions of the druids and bards, often giving hints of the potential future, often kept alive in both collective folklore and individual creativity through the centuries. Thus is ancestral wisdom carried into the future.

To give the reader a poetic or inspired sense of the bards and druids, to share the beauty, terror and wisdom, we have used a wide range of material. Beginning with short summaries of the history of the druids and bards themselves, we include poems, tales, songs, aphorisms, texts and commentaries. An academic textual or archaeological approach is not sufficient on its own, while an absence of such essential disciplines often causes the student or reader to lose context, to be misled or to fantasize excessively. These three losses of truth were known to the bards, who warned against them, and left us a body of traditional lore that was built, like a vehicle, to carry us from the known into the unknown, from the myth into the mystery.

But the bardic vehicle is not dogma, not a set of rules or texts once known to druids and now incomplete or lost. There never was a complete system of druidic wisdom, for it was taught that completion comes first within one's self, through inner change, and only then through a new relationship to universal truth, being or consciousness. So the material handed down is organic, interlaced, a holism of traditions, teachings and initiatory potential experiences.

Forget about wise elders with authoritarian 'druid' teachings, for they never existed other than in the fantasies of repressed Victorian patriarchs (many of whom seem to be still with us today in a variety of thin disguises). Instead of seeking the false grail of dogma or restoration of 'complete systems', do what the bards and druids did, do as the people in the tales, poems and songs do . . . plunge in, unconditionally. Plunge into the depths of the unknown to seek whatever may be found there. Some of those riches, greater than gold or fleeting treasures, are gathered in this book. You will find your own treasures and truths, and the old arts of the druids and bards were designed to help us with such a quest.

R. J. Stewart and Robin Williamson

The Druidic Universe

INTRODUCTION

DRUIDS

R. J. Stewart

The Britons live in the same manner as the ancients, for they fight in chariots as did the ancestral heroes of Greece during the Trojan wars . . . They are straightforward and honest in their business deals, unlike our crafty subtle countrymen . . . The island of Britain is densely populated . . . The Britons always keep their doors open and welcome strangers to eat with them. Only when the feasting is over do they ask who the guests might be and on what business they come.

Diodorus Siculus (*c.* 60 BC)

ho and what were the druids? Our information comes from three distinct sources, described in detail below, and they do not always agree with one another. First, there are the early literary descriptions from the historians and politicians of the ancient world, Greek and Roman. Then there are the poetry, tales and folklore of the Celtic world, preserved in early literature and, from the most ancient of times to the present day, in oral tradition. The third concerns the romantic revival of druidism, which began in the eighteenth century and has not ceased to flourish right up to the present day in various forms. All three sources are supported or challenged by the evidence of archaeology in various ways, and archaeologists draw upon the three sources extensively, though with differing interpretations and emphasis.

There is a wide range of interconnection between our three sources, and it is not always easy for the general reader to see from where information originates. Classical and folkloric sources are often quoted and merged with romantic – that is, fabricated and unauthentic – material in texts from the eighteenth century onwards, and this fabrication continues in popular books and so-called courses in mail-order revival druidism to the present day. While we can easily detect New Age druidism (often commercially linked to New Age shamanism, as distinct from true cultural shamanism) and so dismiss it or accept it according to our taste, discrimination is more difficult when we read texts from before the turn of the century.

Many of the early revivalists, from the eighteenth and nineteenth centuries, fabricated druidic lore. Some also seem to have had contact with genuine oral tradition, in Wales and Brittany in particular. This protean unorganized oral tradition, like that of Gaelic faery lore, was preserved in a diffuse manner well into the twentieth century among rural communities. Part of our exploration in this book is to trace the flow of druid and bardic lore from its mysterious prehistoric, pre-druidic sources, through the historical

The Celtic thunder god, sometimes called Taranis in Latin inscriptions from Gaul

A woodcut of an Irish feast with a harper and story-teller, circa sixteenth century

centuries into a living oral tradition that extends into the present century. This oral tradition, sadly, has all but collapsed within the last two generations.

Classical Literature

The classical sources most often quoted are Julius Caesar, writing on the Gallic Wars in Celtic Europe; Tacitus, describing the Roman attack on Anglesey, off north Wales; Pliny, who describes druid philosophy and ceremonial; and a number of other late Roman historians. The passages in Caesar are woven into a justification of his illegal (officially unapproved) invasion of Gaul, and while he describes Celtic deities and religious practices in Roman terms, there is often a propagandist element. Fortunately for Caesar, though not for the Celts, he was successful in his invasion, and so was voted state support and approval after the event.

The account in Tacitus, probably the most direct, is a simple description of druid priests and priestesses on the sacred island of Anglesey and of the Roman soldiers' initial fear and subsequent blood lust. The entire centre of druidic training on Anglesey was destroyed, and the men and women massacred. As Tacitus is describing what was found in a remote but major druid training school and sacred island at a specific date (AD 61) his text gives us a clear, if miniature picture. Furthermore, Tacitus is supported by some of the archaeological finds from a haul in the lake of Llyn Cerrig Bach on Anglesey, where a substantial ritual treasure hoard has been found.

Pliny deals more with the magical and mystical rites of the druids as they were popularly described in his own time: he is not

reporting something he witnessed but elaborating upon the words of others. By the time much of Celtic Europe had been assimilated into the Roman Empire, druids enjoyed a fashionable vogue similar to that enjoyed today by Native Americans among white New Age enthusiasts. The druids, once the scourge of Roman might, once capable of whipping Celtic warriors into attack and revolt, eventually became a popularized source of natural wisdom. This natural wisdom may or may not have been connected to true druid tradition, just as New Age enthusiasm for tribal lore, so-called shamanism, and (more recently) Australian aboriginal beliefs, may or may not ring true today.

Celtic Tradition and Its Literature

Traditional sources in Celtic culture, both written and oral, contain a substantial but often contradictory collection of information on druids and bards. Irish druids, for example, seem to have been different from Welsh druids, and though interpreters from Roman times to the present day have assumed that druidism was a pan-European religious structure, there is no clear evidence for this. Indeed, Celtic sources make it clear that druidism was diverse and non-centralized, and that it underwent many changes through a period of several centuries. Many of the statements about organized or systematic druidism in twentieth-century literature derive (either as information or in attitude) from eighteenth- and nineteenth-century literary sources and are not supported by the evidence of Celtic oral tradition, Celtic literature, or archaeology.

Before we explore the field of literature from Celtic tradition that mentions druids, we must be utterly clear on one significant truth. None of the Celtic source literature is by druids. There is no genuine historic druidic literature whatsoever. Bardic sources are explored on pages 16–17, and although we are certain that the lore of the bards incorporates much of the later (post-Roman period) traditions and wisdom teachings of the druids, there is no 'proof' of this in the sense of literary history and traceable documents linking the bards and druids.

The reason for this is simple, though frustrating for the modern reader. Druid teachings and practices were strictly oral: nothing was written down. Indeed, writing was unknown in Celtic societies and territories until after contact with, and colonization by, the Romans. Although much has been made of the ogham system of inscription in recent years, this is not an ancient druidic alphabet. Ogham inscriptions on stones are usually in crude Latin, and are not likely to be earlier than the second century AD. Ogham certainly developed into several branches up to as late as the eleventh century, not as an alphabet for writing texts but as a mnemonic system for keying into vast areas of memorized or regenerative poetry, imagery, genealogies and other oral lore. It is highly likely that various kinds of ogham were used as keys for memory even by Celtic poets who

Druidesses cursing Roman soldiers at Anglesey

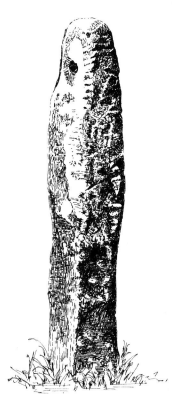

A standing stone, with ogham *incisions on edges*

could both read and write in Latin, Greek and their own native languages.

We must think of all druid lore as preserved in memory and handed down through strict discipline and training of the mind. There were no druid books and even after the spread of the Roman and Greek alphabets, and of writing in monastic centres, any surviving druidic or bardic poetic lore was not handed on by written instruction.

Fortunately, some of the oral tradition was written down, and it is from such sources, dating from the medieval period in Ireland and Wales, that we have some genuine (though non-systematic) druid teachings. Written material began with monastic scribes, who formalized a huge body of oral poetry and tales. This oral tradition was alive and active at the time that the monks transcribed it, and they wrote it out either from personal knowledge or from the recital of poets and story-tellers within their own culture.

Thus in Ireland we have mention of druids, combined with many pagan magical themes and practices, in the epics of ancient queens, kings, heroes, battles and so forth. There is also a distinct body of literature serving as propaganda *against* the druids to be found in monastic political texts, such as lives of the saints, histories and chronicles. This is distinct because its aim is propagandist and negative, while the early texts of oral poetry and tales are clearly from a pagan world, even though Christian ideas and dogma occur from time to time.

In Wales we have material from the sixth century AD onwards in both Latin and old Welsh. Many druidic ideas, particularly those on cosmology and prophecy, were assembled into Latin texts, both prose and poetry, by Geoffrey of Monmouth. The cosmology and prophecy are closely linked by Geoffrey to the figure of Merlin, who is a generic person, standing for a body of bardic and druidic lore in Wales and Lowland Scotland. No large body of lore exists in writing before Geoffrey, though there are other chronicles that seem to have drawn upon similar sources for legendary history.

By the sixteenth century, some collections of bardic tales and poems were preserved in Welsh as handwritten books alongside the various written genealogies and chronicles in Welsh or Latin. The most famous of these is the collection known as the *Mabinogion*, which includes many mythic and magical themes. Many of the poetic traditions of the bards, such as the famous 'Triads' and 'Taliesin' poems were also written down from oral tradition during this crucial transition period, though some material dates from earlier written sources.

The transition from oral to literate was limited, however, to the ruling classes, who sought to have written material prepared for them by professional scribes and poets. The oral tradition of the non-literate Celts (in all Celtic countries and languages) continued to be unbroken.

The 'Triads' are examples of druidic/bardic mnemonics. They are short lists of threefold truths or significant events. They were a type of menu or index to the accumulated lore of the oral tradition as preserved by specialist training. In other words, you used the 'Triads' as a checklist for what you knew, though this is only the most superficial level of their use.

To give the reader some idea of the vast size of collections of Welsh bardic/druidic lore in early literature, we can look at the material in the British Museum. Manuscripts in old Welsh (known as the Myrvyrian MSS) contain over 4,000 poems and 2,000 epigrams, and amount to thousands of pages of handwritten texts. The same collection includes later prose sources from the seventeenth and eighteenth centuries that seem to contain a mass of material copied and extrapolated from oral tradition. These texts are in 53 volumes, totalling over 15,000 pages.

Extract from The Red Book of Hergest *('The Mabinogion')*

There are many other manuscripts in collections in libraries and museums and in private ownership, and the examples just mentioned are offered simply because they are among the best known (see pages 30–39 for more detailed descriptions of this particular material).

In Ireland the amount of poetic/druidic material in manuscripts, both translated and untranslated, is substantial. Many enthusiasts are unaware that modern popular books on Celtic tradition draw on very limited resources, as the bulk of the source material is still unpublished, still untranslated.

Revival Druidism

Romantic revivals of druidism range from wildly exotic theories about the lost tribes of Israel and the priesthood of sunken Atlantis to attempts to weld together selected material from Celtic and classical sources with a patriarchal Judaeo-Christian worldview. This is not new, of course, for the early Christians were obliged to do the same as they evangelized regions in which druidism was a major feature of the culture. More recently, revivals of druidism in Europe and the USA have lost the dogmatic Christian flavour, preferring paganism, but retained the dogmatic patriarchal Victorian systematic approach. This systematic and rigid mental stance (often said to be a philosophy) is absent from Celtic tradition and is a relatively modern idea.

Contemporary romantic 'druidism' has no connection to druidic tradition, other than through intellectual systematic restatements of relatively modern sources, which in themselves dealt with druidic and bardic material at many removes from Celtic culture.

There is a stronger case to be made, however, for the validity of Welsh druidic material from the eighteenth and nineteenth centuries, for in some cases the writers tapped into an oral tradition in addition to interpreting literary sources. There are strong poetic traditions in Wales, preserved and kept alive through small meetings which over the centuries handed down druidic and more specifically bardic lore in a diffuse but living way – not as literature or historic re-creation, but as a living tradition of ideas, poetic forms, images and teachings. This oral tradition, which gave rise to the nationalistic revival of the *eisteddfod* in the nineteenth century, was tapped into by writers such as Iolo Morgannwg (see page 116).

We shall return to the important links between druids and bards in tradition later. For the present, it is sufficient to say that in practice druids and bards became indistinguishable from one another at a very early date, and that our modern attitude in writing about them separately is in many ways misleading. There is no parallel revival of druidism in Ireland that matches the Welsh, which is perhaps due to the influence of the Catholic Church, which consistently absorbed old traditions.

Druids and Romans

The Emperor Tiberius made the first state decree against the druids, who share this unusual honour with the early Christians. Contrary to popular opinion, the Roman state was remarkably liberal in religious matters and allowed wide freedom of worship. This liberality was fundamental to the ancient world, and the idea of conflicting religions only developed with the absorption of Judaic laws into developing Christianity. In time the religious ideas of simplicity and purity of worship became political propaganda.

Both early Christians and druids were proscribed, declared illegal, for one basic reason. They were regarded as terrorists. During

A relief carving of a Romano-Celtic deity, sometimes called Esv

Triple-hooded deities, from Housesteads Roman fort, Northumberland

the reign of Nero, the Christians increasingly refused to make the statutory acknowledgements to the emperor, though these acknowledgements were openly known to be political tokens of allegiance and not true worship. Thus the Christians were the equivalent of any extremist group today that openly defies all legal authority.

The druids, however, were a more complex problem. Tiberius fastened on to the propaganda originated by Julius Caesar and Suetonius Paulinus that druids practised human sacrifice, which had been banned a century or so earlier in Rome. But the truth was that druids from Britain frequently travelled in secret to Gaul (mainland Europe) to foment rebellion.

Diogenes Laertius wrote that the druids had three main ideals: to revere Divine Being, to abstain from evil and to live with courage. This triad, quoted by a Roman writer, is typical of the traditional 'Triads' (see pages 26–29), which held the foundations of bardic and druidic lore.

Some Conclusions

What we know of the druids, therefore comes from diverse and contradictory sources, with many overlays of uncertain origin and truthfulness. If we were to list a minimal definition of druidism, it would include two main points:

1 Druidism is not a sect or a single religion but a philosophy arising at a relatively late period, and suppressed in its prime by Roman imperialism, out of the diverse Celtic and pre-Celtic religions. This philosophy, which embraced all aspects of universal awareness, physical and metaphysical, was developed and presented by specifically trained orders, within a caste of what we might today call priests and priestesses. Such definitions are used with caution and reserve, as druids merged several functions that are nowadays quite separate.

The druids were an aristocratic group or caste, with hereditary roles in some cases but admitting members for training in others. As a historical movement druidism was diverse, with regional and national variations, yet it encompassed Celtic religion and at its height of power controlled many aspects of religious and civic life.

Druidism might be likened to a 'New Religious Philosophy' of the Celts, a set of dominant, highly refined beliefs and practices that was the culmination of wisdom and experience laid down over thousands of years by the Celts and the pre-Celtic peoples of Europe. This long-term foundation and background to druidism could be likened to an 'Old Religion', though it was a holism of many religions rather than an organized single unit.

2 Druidism was specifically concerned with knowledge, both exoteric and esoteric. The exoteric knowledge included history and genealogy, healing, astronomy/astrology, geography and preserving and disseminating the arts and skills for which the Celts were famous throughout the ancient world, as well as the arts of design and proportion, including geometry and architecture (though these are modern terms that have lost their original sacred meaning). In exoteric knowledge, the druid orders were a vast storehouse of all that was known to the Celts, and this included much from the Greeks, the Phoenicians and other civilizations.

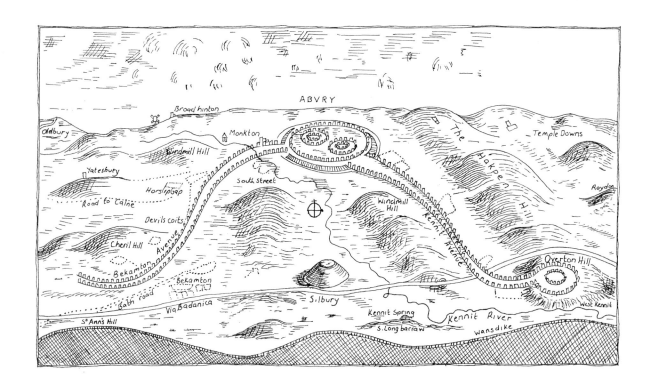

A standing stone engraved with a Celtic deity

Esoteric knowledge was not separated from exoteric, as it is today. History and genealogy, preserved entirely in memory as poems and epics, were also the keys to ancestral power and magic, to the life story of the land and its people. Healing was done with herbs and minerals, and included bone-setting and the sewing of battle wounds; but it also involved invoking deities, use of subtle life energies, and the primal concept and technique of working with spirit or faery allies. Variants of this ancestral magical therapy were preserved in faery healing right into the twentieth century in folk tradition.

Astronomy/astrology formed a major theme in druidism, probably inherited and developed from the astronomical observations and alignments of the earlier megalithic cultures, whose people built the stone alignments and mounds traditionally associated with druids. Although these structures pre-date druids by thousands of years in some cases, the tradition is so well preserved in each century that we may conclude that the druids used the ancient stone circles and alignments, though they certainly did not build them.

The civilized skills such as astronomy link to geography and the arts of navigation, and skills in craftwork were widely employed not only for trade and personal adornments but as part of religious ceremony. Archaeologists have found huge hoards of ornate gold and metalwork, jewellery, arms, chariots and ritual scale models of objects, none of which was intended for anything other than ceremonial use and sacrifice. It seems likely that the druids had

Left: *A romantic reconstruction of Avebury by Stukeley, 1740*

Right: *A reconstruction of Avebury from a nineteenth-century engraving*

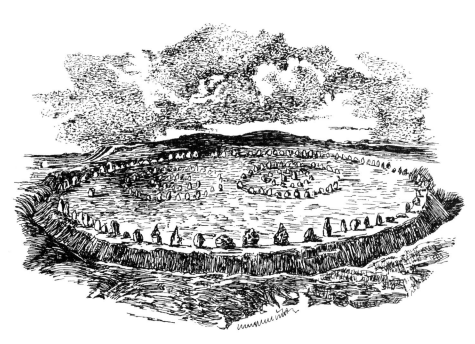

a strong association with the artistic crafts as well as the poetic and prophetic arts, and this is supported equally by Celtic written and oral tradition.

Druids also preserved and disseminated the cultural skills associated with a high population (as attested by classical historians, who describe Britain as densely populated and having many tribal centres or 'cities'). The main concern of this branch of druidic wisdom was the mirroring of a metaphysical ideal into the social order. A classic example of this is the unifying of ancient Ireland according to the sacred directions, with specific castes and functions in the east, south, west, and north, with the high king and the court in the centre. This social caste pattern mirrored on earth the metaphysical or magical pattern of the sacred directions in other dimensions, as described in a number of Irish texts.

In this context of geomantic relativity we also find the druidic arts of architecture, which consisted of bringing balance and vitality to dwelling places through design, orientation, decoration and the use of appropriate materials. A contemporary equivalent might be the Chinese traditional art of *feng shui*, inherited from ancient times. A number of Irish sources give emphasis to the proper structure and placement of dwellings, in keeping with the sacred directions.

Most of all, druids were associated with prophecy, judgement and rectitude or right living. Thus the senior druids attended and advised the kings and queens, who were in turn responsible, often with their lives, for the welfare of the land and the tribes or nations.

The themes of prophecy, judgement (bringing justice) and rectitude (virtue) also play an important role in the idea of initiatory or transformative arts and disciplines. Just as the druidic knowledge was applied to the tribe, land or state, it could also be used individually for personal and spiritual growth. The druid training was often reported (from classical times onward) to last 20 years. Some of the time was spent acquiring the repertoire, the lists, poems, genealogies, sets of laws, aphorisms and so forth. Some was spent in practical 'hands-on' skills, ranging from work with substance and matter to healing and advising others. A great deal of the druidic training involved a combination of trance, visionary work, prophetic arts and ritual magic.

At this stage we are not making the customary threefold division of bards, vates and judges, or bards, ovates and druids, so popular with modern writers. To be a druid, the individual had to have knowledge of many skills and arts, and some branches of the tradition seem to have worked through the three orders or initiatory levels. In the Welsh orders of druidism, the bards were originally, but not exclusively, preservers and creators of poetic knowledge in many oral forms. The *vates* were prophets, often with the additional connotations of madness, wildness and itinerant randomness. Druids were judges, called in to define decisions and custom among the nobility.

Druids at standing stones in Callanish in the Hebrides

The entrance to New Grange, a prehistoric ritual chamber in Ireland

This threefold pattern is found in the *Vita Merlini* by Geoffrey of Monmouth, where Merlin is first a young noble (not a bard), then a mad prophet, running with the wild animals, and finally a wise elder who is revered by the Welsh princes but refuses to judge on their behalf, preferring instead to withdraw into spiritual contemplation. The bardic role in this exposition of druidic/bardic lore, written out in Latin in 1193, is taken by the other popular figure from Welsh tradition, Taliesin.

In the *Vita*, Taliesin is a bard who recites and teaches universal knowledge of the three worlds: Overworld, Middle World (that of our planetary life) and Underworld (see figure on page 10). In the 'Taliesin' texts, however, we find him as a developing initiate, advancing within the druidic mysteries of both magical and of spiritual transformation.

It might be argued that the later Welsh, Irish and Breton texts and collections from oral tradition are not druidic. Strictly speaking this is true, for the druids ceased to exist formally at some time during the third and fourth centuries AD, and, as we have already seen, they preserved all of their lore orally, by memory, without written sources. Yet it seems certain that much of druidic tradition was handed down through the centuries via lineages of bards in Brittany, Wales and Lowland Scotland, and of poets in Ireland. Chroniclers of various kinds also wrote down the lore of the bards or poets from the tenth century onwards, without necessarily being trained themselves (though some seem to have been taught many aspects of the traditions that they reported).

It has also been argued that all magical or initiatory themes in Celtic tradition are confused relics of a once coherent druidic system. This cannot be true, as such coherence did not exist within the druid orders themselves, as evidenced by the differences between Irish and British (Scots and Welsh) druidic traditions, and between the Lowland and Highland Scots traditions. The idea of rigid systems and complete patterns is a materialist one, that of the universal machine, the clockwork model, deriving from the eighteenth and nineteenth centuries. It does not exist in nature but solely in the minds of people who need the false authority of a 'complete system' or 'hierarchy' to bolster them up.

What is most likely is that the druids, and later the bards and poets, took the mass of magical, mythic and mystical lore found at all levels of Celtic culture and refined certain practices for special-ized applications. The religious themes, the folk magic and the echoes of ancient pre-Celtic and then tribal and national Celtic divinities all continued within a massive collective stream of tradi-tion. Thus items within that stream were neither strictly druidic nor non-druidic, but organically linked to the refined arts and sciences, to the specialized practices, of the varied druid orders in different Celtic countries.

BARDS

Robin Williamson

Among the Celts are honoured poets called bards who to the music of harps (instruments like lyres) chant praise of some, satire of others. Also they have philosophers called druids whom they hold in high veneration. Prophets they have also who foretell future events.

Diodorus Siculus (*c.* 60 BC)

The earliest texts mentioning druids talk of the esteem in which poets were held. In the very diverse tribal and highly localized Britain of the pre-Christian era, different regions tended to have their own particular gods and goddess, associated with wells, rivers and hills, with the landscape generally and with the heavens. They had local customs, some of which persist to our own time. It seems that there was a formalized druidic or bardic philosophy held in common throughout Britain from the early years of the Christian era until the fifth or sixth century AD. It is from just after this time that the earliest bardic records are dated.

It is likely that pre-Celtic stone monuments continued to be revered, with or without the sanction of the pagan or Christianized druids. The Celtic Christian Church incorporated a great deal of Celtic druidry. In many places the druids became priests without missing a step. Druidic ideas are mentioned in Christian texts together with lore of herbs and trees, properties of wells, sacred hills and reverence for the sun, the moon and the sea, as well as for the crowned babe and his mother.

We have, in the traditions we inherit, folk-song, music and dance, folk customs and superstitions, traditional remedies, folk witchcraft and seasonal rituals, and it is likely, given the retentive nature of human culture, that all of these contain strands of druidic and pre-druidic usage.

Many of the early Celtic Christian saints were male or female bards as well as clerics. As Christianity developed in Britain, druidry ceased gradually to be the dominant religion. The power focus associated with monarchy became Christian in context. The bards, however, continued to wield semi-druidical powers of blessing and cursing, praise and satire, well into the Middle Ages. Throughout the medieval period, bards were the advisers of kings and nobles. High bards in particular are differentiated from lower ones in Britain:

High-degree bardic practice *Prydyddiaeth*
Family harper practice *Teulwriaeth*
Travelling minstrel practice *Clerwriaeth*

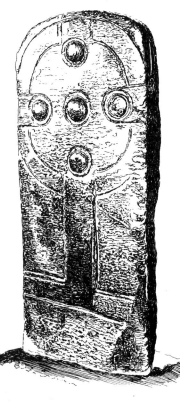

A Celtic cross, showing the connection of worlds

A crwth, *an old Welsh bowed lyre, used extensively by itinerant musicians and story-tellers*

Bards of high degree in Britain were recognized as having undergone an initiation into the mysteries of the art under the patronage of the goddess Ceridwen.

The magical poetic traditions of Britain and Ireland developed independently and have different though comparable features. The term bard in Ireland was not complimentary. The Irish word for a poet was *fili*; a master poet was called *ollamh*. British heritage is preserved in what is now called Wales, though prior to the Anglo-Saxon and Viking invasions of the sixth to ninth centuries AD, Welsh was spoken throughout Britain as far north as central Scotland. Two of the best-known early British Celtic bards were northern: Aneurin, author of the earliest known Welsh poem, 'Gododdin', lived in what is now Edinburgh, and Taliesin, the most famous of all, bard to King Urien of Rheged, lived near what is now Carlisle. Merlin, or Myrddin, has a southern Scottish as well as Welsh and Breton associations. It must be remembered that although some of the finest Celtic and pre-Celtic sites are to be found in what is now England, traditional Celtic philosophy and lore have been preserved almost entirely in Wales, Ireland and Scotland. In these countries the bardic tradition of poetic power remained long after it was lost in England. The lore of the bards has been preserved in a tradition from the Welsh heritage of ideas which were grouped in threes, the *Triads of the Island of Britain*.

Strata Florida Abbey, near Aberystwyth, North Wales, the site of the grave of Dafyyd ap Gwilym

Poetic Power

Three things that make a bard:
Playing of the harp
Knowledge of ancient lore
Poetic power.

What is this poetic power that is so often asserted? Why would one study the legends of one's ancestry? Why does one ply words with words and construct notes upon notes of tunes? It is stated repeatedly that there is power to be won here not available in ordinary school; not for sale in colleges. Only one who yearns for poetry with feet made for journeys will get a taste of it. The Gaelic word for poem or song is *dan*, which really means not only song but also skill and destiny. It includes the notions of praising and foretelling and, more importantly, magical power over the article or person so treated.

Poetry is made of the quality of mist and starlight, of every untouchable thing. Is it a mesh to trap the mincing mind till the soul leaps free one moment. Legends, songs: a lifetime to learn them, many lifetimes to learn them all, many years to understand one tune and many tellings to understand one story.

Knowing what has happened upon a hill, why a river has a certain name, the meaning of a stone in a field – these are histories that make everyday surroundings magical. This knowledge is a crossing of waters. But the power to tell a story that never happened in the world at all, that is an enchantment; that suspends time and care. It takes the hard mile after the easy mile and the mountain above the hill to do that.

What is a word? A sound only. What is its meaning? It means what it means as it is heard, as it is thought, as it is said. The bards were seeking and were worshipping the invisible power behind language. They sought the connections between things. Does a star affect a herb? Can a herb cure a sickness? Does a word affect a star? Can a whistle raise a storm?

Stepping out of the door of one's own house, one carries the weather in one's head; the history of one's view of the entire universe; memories that haze as days recede. One who wishes to attain understanding seeks to survive the poison, the fact of death. Seeks to leave signs and messages for those who will come later. Sees poetry as a kind of prayer, a kind of teacher. Knows that poetry is not made of words but out of bones and gardens, winter rain, kisses and whatnot. Knows that it is not only found on pages but met upon mountains, eaten in fruit, drunk in strong drink. Poetry is caused by love. It is a sculpture of one's own life.

These ideas are, I believe, the traditional British approach to the mystery of art.

William Williams, Wil Penmorfa, *the blind Welsh harpist, 1759–1828*

THE BIRTH OF TALIESIN

BEFORE THE EAGLE married the owl, there was a woman of power and her name was Ceridwen. Her daughter Creirwy had beauty that put shame to the wild rose, but her son Afagddu was the ugliest and wickedest boy in the world and the dark night of December was too bright for him. Ceridwen knew there was no way forward for Afagddu unless he could excel in wit or wisdom. But in these, as in all else, he was sadly lacking.

Ceridwen consulted the learning of the ages and she compounded the spell for a cauldron of inspiration that would make Afagddu wise. She gathered together wheat, honey, incense, myrrh, aloes, precious silver and fluxwort. She set the brew to boil in a virgin cauldron. To boil one year and one day.

She hired a servant boy, Gwion Bach, to keep that cauldron at the boil, to stir it slow, to keep it from boiling dry. Eight months and nine months he was at that very work, till one morning near the year's end, three drops splashed on the back of his hand while he was stirring, and seeking to cool the scalded flesh, he knew at once the past, the present and the future. He knew then also that Ceridwen meant his death. He took to his heels, out of the door, while the cauldron cracked in pieces behind him. For all the liquid intended for Afagddu was in those three drops and all the liquid that remained was the deadliest poison.

When Ceridwen heard the crack of the cauldron, she was quick to make after him. Gwion became a hare for speed, but she became a black greyhound bitch and hounded him ever the closer. He became a salmon and through the waters, but she became an otter and after him ever the closer. He became a dove and through the air, but she became a hawk and after him ever the closer. In the last failing of his strength, he became a groat of wheat in a pile of wheat in a barnyard, but she became a black hen and pecked and scuffed in the pile of wheat till she found the one groat that was Gwion Bach, pecked him up and swallowed him down.

But if all is true that is no lie, that was not the end of him, for Ceridwen bore another son in the course of time and that son was Gwion Bach. But such a lovely baby as he was now, she had not the heart to kill him outright, but she bound him into a bag of skins and cast him into the sea.

The sea swept up, the sea swept down, the sea danced after the light moon and the dark, from the time of King Arthur until the time of Maelgwn Gwynedd, and that was a long time. But the babe aged not one day in that bag or in that time. Until finally one May eve that bag was caught in the salmon nets of a king called Gwyddno near what is now Aberystwyth.

Every year King Gwyddno was in the habit of granting the salmon rights to one he wished to favour. And this year it was to his own son Elffin he gave the fishing rights.

A bit of a wastrel, a bit of a spendthrift young Elffin was, so they say, and he badly needed the worth of those salmon to pay his gambling debts. He wasn't long in wading out to where the nets were pegged across the river mouth , where he could see a black something bobbing in the current midstream. He dragged it ashore. Maybe it was something of value, a cask of drink, a box of jewels. He opened it up.

Out jumped the babe from the mouth of the bag, speaking words of poetry and power the likes of which had never been heard in the world before. And because of the light that streamed from the baby's face, Elffin gave him the name Taliesin, which means 'shining brow'. They went back together to Gwyddno's hall.

Gwyddno looked up as they came in. 'I hope you caught plenty of fish!'

'Better than that, father. I caught a poet.'

It was then that Taliesin spoke these words, as the bards relate:

I am Taliesin
I sing perfect metre which will last until the world's end
I know why an echo answers again
Why liver is bloody, why breath is without colour, why silver
   shines
I know why a cow has horns
And why a woman loves a man
Why milk is white and holly green
Ale bitter and ocean brine
How many spears make a confrontation
How many drops make a shower of rain
I know why there are scales on fish and black feet on swans.

I have been a blue salmon
A dog, a stag, a roebuck on the mountain
A stick, a spade, an axe in the hand
A buck, a bull, a stallion
Upon a hill I was grown as grain
Reaped and in the oven thrown
Out of that roasting I fell to the ground
Pecked up and swallowed by the black hen
In her crop nine nights lain
I have been dead, I have been alive
I am Taliesin

(English version by Robin Williamson)

This medieval story can be taken as a folklore description of the initiation of bards. The steps are as follows:

Step 1 Stirring the Cauldron
As I have just outlined, this involves learning the material and takes however long it takes.

Step 2 Animal Transformations and Pursuit by the Muse
This must have to do with self-knowledge, only to be acquired in life, in the understanding of one's strengths and weaknesses, and results in the acquisition not so much of a new name as one's original name. It has to do with the acquisition of one's own voice.

Step 3 Casting Adrift
Having surrendered to the powers of the infinite and taken part in the song of life, one emerges after a kind of triple birth, three times as alive.

The Three Worlds

Underlying all manifestation is the world called Annwn. In this world is found the island fortress called Caer Siddi, where rests the perfect chair of the bards: 'neither age nor sorrow corrupts him who sits in it'. Also in Annwn are the cauldron of inspiration and rebirth, and the springs of the water of life.

The world in which we live is called Abred. It is intersected at every point by Annwn, from which all life proceeds.

The currently unimaginable completeness to which all things are ultimately destined is called Gwynwyd:

> There is no anger which will not at last be pacified
> There is nothing beloved lost which will not at last be returned
> There is no soul born which will not at last attain the perfection
>   of Gwynwyd.

The Gorsedd

The Welsh word *gorsedd* means a chair or a gathering of bards. The motto of the chair of the bards of Britain is: *Y Gwir yn erbyn y byd* (Truth against the world).

> THE GORSEDD PRAYER
> Grant, O God, Thy refuge
> And in refuge, strength
> And in strength, understanding
> And in understanding, knowledge
> And in knowledge, perception of rightness
> And in perception of rightness, the love of it
> And in that love, the love of all existences
> And in the love of all existences, the love of God.

This ancient poem from the Welsh heritage is attributed to the early bard Talhairn. It is used in assemblies of the bards and druids of Britain to this day.

An early prose translation of the medieval poem called 'The Chair of Taliesin' has this to say about the initiation of bards:

> The person of complete understanding obtains the drink of honour in every lordly gathering. Then the most high is worshipped with offerings of wheat, honey, myrrh and aloes from beyond the waters, with the golden pipes of Lleu, with silver, ruddy gem, berries and ocean foam, river cresses and vervain.

What is being referred to is the preparation of the cauldron of inspiration as made by Ceridwen for her son Afagddu, whose name means dark wings.

Possibly some actual libation was drunk in the first ceremonies of the initiation of bards: the gold pipes of Lleu are possibly broom flowers; the fluxwort known in Wales as *ariant Gwion* – Gwion's silver; the ruddy gem perhaps the hedge berry known as *eirin Gwion* or Borues of Gwion; the cresses called *fabaria*, called *berwr Taliesin* or Taliesin's cresses; and the vervain gathered at the time of the rising of Sirius, 'without being looked upon by either the sun or the moon', and gathered with the left hand, with propitiation to the earth of a gift of honey.

Whatever these herbal activities, initiation into the rites of Ceridwen was still common in Christian Britain in the twelfth century and is mentioned in a poem by the Welsh prince Hywel at that date.

The Awen

Repeatedly referred to in the bardic writings is lore relative to the origins of the alphabet, its relationship to trees and the secret name of God.

> Writing was invented by Einiged the giant, son of Alser, for the purpose of recording praiseworthy deeds.
> They were first carved on wooden staves called coel bren.
> The first three letters were obtained by Menw the Aged, who observed light falling in three rays.

This is the sign known as Awen, which is said to be the name by which the universe calls God inwardly. The Awen is said to represent the letters OIU, from which all others are obtained. The O relates to the perfect circle of Gwynwyd, the I to the mortal world, Abred, and the U to the cauldron of Annwn. They relate to earth, sea and air; body, mind and spirit; and love, wisdom and truth. The word Awen also means not only this combination of letters but inspiration and soul as well.

> The three foundations of Awen are:
> To understand truth
> To love truth
> To maintain truth.

It is said: 'No one without Awen from God can pronounce these three letters correctly.'

HU GADARN AND THE AFANC

WHEN BABEL FELL and language cracked, across the flood came sailing Hu Gadarn, the son of the sun. He brought the two first oxen, the oxen of the sun, into the Island of the Mighty, the sacred island of Britain. Hu Gadarn came to the pool in Dyfed where the monster lived that was the Child of Darkness, the Afanc. It was because of the Afanc that the lake of floods burst forth and drowned the world. Hu Gadarn with his oxen drew the Afanc from the waters so the lake of floods burst forth no more. He put a chain about the Afanc that binds it still.

When I lived in west Wales in the 1960s this fragment about Hu Gadarn was current folklore in the region; older people would refer to a certain pool where this binding of the Afanc occurred. Many that I spoke to then, farmers and other country people, felt that Welsh inheritance in druidry (wisdom, magic, healing) and bardism (prophecy, inspiration, mystical direct teaching from the universe itself) were a continuance of matters anciently referred to in the Old Testament. In a way this is true. The ancient mythology of the world before Abraham seems to have held in common a sense of sanctity of landscape. The psalms are very 'bardic', inspired songs sung to the harp. The harp is central to the whole Celtic notion of spoken-word performance and the whole idea of inspiration. Like humanity itself, it evolves from Africa. The modern Welsh word for harp, *telyn*, is related to the ancient Egyptian word for the harp, *teluni*.

All poetry was originally religious in character. Poetry was the first religion, says the ancient Greek author Strabo. Celtic poetry was intended to be chanted, declaimed or sung to the harp. Ceremony, magic and healing are to be understood as part of Celtic poetry and harp music. The healing powers are said in Scottish Gaelic tradition to be capable of soothing a woman in labour or a man with a spear wound. This is illustrated in the following poem, deriving from medieval Gaelic.

IN PRAISE OF THE HARP

Harp of Coscair's fortified height
Bringer of rest to over wakeful eyes
Voice of tunefulness, solemn and bright.

Masterly curved, strong-tongued singer
Red as the patterned leaf of power
To bring us repose by play of skilled fingers

Healer of the wounded, princely in wooing
Brotherly voice over the dark ale flowing
Weaver of charms with persuasive crooning.

(English version by Robin Williamson)

The clumsy harper

But satire and humour were very important in Celtic poetry also. A classic example of this is the following mid-fourteenth-century poem by Dafydd ap Gwilym, in which he contrasts unfavourably the Irish wire-strung harp to the sweet-sounding hair-strung buzzing harp of Wales.

SATIRE ON THE IRISH HARP

Grant, O Great God,
That the luminous melody of Wales
Fail not nor darken
Music we had once
In green fair gardens
Now these sharp tidings bite among us
Noisy strumming dismal
Leather-sided Irish harps

David the prophet
Had not one string from wire nor entrails
But of fine black plaited hair
His strings were made
Now we suffer
Bad luck to it
This leather-sided coffer
From Eire

Shamed to play it
They should be
With their ugly horny nails
A month or more to put in tune
Coppery whore it is
Sorrow to see
Naked bow
It rasps
Like young stumbling crows

Because I thirst for beauty
I love not
Its button-covered belly nor its gut
Its sallow hue
Its gaudy ornament
Its broken-armed angle
Its bent post
Only a villain cares for it

Under the eight playing fingers
Ugly its swollen trough
Its smoky case
Its carcass

Its hoarse voice
Fit only for decrepit English
Its song

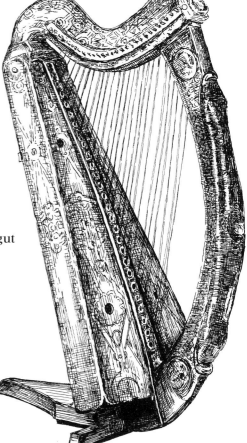

*The oldest surviving
Irish harp, the so-called
Brian Boru harp, from
fifteenth or sixteenth
century*

like the neighing of mares
For the cock horse
Its night disturbance
Sister to the yellow hag of ill

Graceful its metre
As a lame goose through stubble
A squealing foolish Irish witch
Rumbling like the water wheel
Its shriek
Like a rabbit snared by the neck
Wooden sickle for hacking nettles
Tottering shin
Of a crone

Let every real musician
From the Marches to Mona
Learn to play
The right Welsh hair-strung harp
Let such be taught
As in the ancient times
As for this other
Giftless twanging thing
Let no one bear it
In the face of day.

(English version by Robin Williamson)

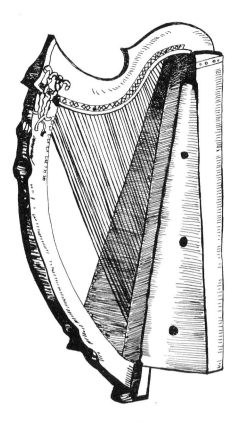

*An early Celtic harp,
from an illustration by
Michael Praetorius*

As already mentioned, Welsh was spoken as far north as central Scotland in the Dark Ages and one of the earliest known Welsh poems, the 'Gododdin', was written in what is now called Edinburgh by the bard Aneurin. He was the bard to Mynyddog Mwyn Fawr, Big-handed Mynyddog, who was king over what is now south-east Scotland, his capital being in the region of the modern-day Edinburgh suburb of Duddingston. Here is an extract from his lament for the defeat of his people by the Angles:

Men went to Catterick,
They were honoured
Their wages they drank from gold cups
In the feasting hall
Year long the minstrelsy
The harp strings never still
Let the blood now that rusts their shields
Never be scoured.

In this verse it is confirmed that warriors were paid in advance with feasting and praise poems.

The Welsh king, Maelgwn Gwynnedd, mentioned in 'The Birth of Taliesin,' greatly favoured bards and harpers, as noted with disapproval by the early monastic historian Gildas.

Traditionally, the Welsh king Gruffydd ap Cynan of Gwynedd, whose mother was Irish, established an agreement on poetic metres and musical theory between the Irish and the Welsh in about 1100. The earliest actual texts of music for the Welsh harp, however, are found only in one precious manuscript.

The Ap Huw Manuscript

Robert ap Huw was probably a court musician to King James I. He achieved the title Pen Cerdd, chief musician, at the Caerwys Eisteddfod in 1567. His manuscript, which dates from about 1613, is the earliest known Celtic music manuscript in general and describes what is surely a medieval if not an earlier system for the harp. He goes into great detail about the many metres of music, various tunings, stresses of root chord against one other chord, and many detailed fingering of ornaments and stopped notes. It is clear that his is a method for accompanying story-telling and song in a style of theme and variation similar to pibroch (in Scottish piping) and akin in some ways to bell-ringing.

This older music did not persist into the repertoire of eighteenth-century musicians. It was replaced by European dance styles, by Irish, English and Scottish popular dance styles, and by the music of the English theatre. The Welsh gentry from the sixteenth century onwards were either increasingly anglicized or already English, as in Ireland and Scotland, where the older aristocracy was replaced and in proportion the patronage of bards declined.

The Welsh poetic styles of Cywyddau, complex praise poetry, could not be performed properly without the ancient harp playing in accompaniment.

No other manuscript clues to the early bardic style survive in either Ireland or Scotland other than certain beautiful melodies noted by Edward Bunting in the eighteenth century from the work of the aged Irish harp player Dennis Hempson and from a number of surviving pieces by the Scottish seventeenth-century harper-poet Rory Dal Morison, who was related to my father's ancestors, the Robertsons of Glen Shee.

The famous Welsh harper John Parry (1710–82) played and wrote eighteenth-century-style music but also published Welsh traditional dance tunes and mentions an older style of *penillion* singing different from what was then current in which the singer improvises a melody across a traditional tune. The earlier practice as noted consisted of fitting original words about a traditional melody, improvised upon by a harper. This practice was also remarked upon by Edward Jones, *bardd y brennin*, who published his highly influential *Musical and Poetickal Reliques of the Welsh Bards* in 1784.

Three of equal rank:
A king, a harper and a bard.

*The Queen Mary harp,
a fifteenth-century
Scottish harp*

The aristocratic bardic musical and poetic traditions, however, were not the only influences at work in Celtic culture. The oral heritage of folk-song, folk-dance and folk-legend, which contains much of the mother lode of truth available in more refined art, inspired and invigorated everything. In the same way, the earliest wonder tales of Irish tradition persisted alongside the changing literary heritage, and continue into the twentieth century, long after more formal romance or saga had declined.

> A harper, one who has love for his country, ought to be well averst with the history of his country and to be acquainted with the mountains, valleys, rocks, rivers, dingles and dales, so as to be able to give a true sound to his national music.
>
> John Roberts, Welsh Harper

The Romany gypsy tradition of harping was represented in Wales by the descendants of the eighteenth-century practitioner Abram Woods. Many of the Woodses and the Robertses were famous harpers in the nineteenth century.

PART ONE

The Cauldron
◆
Wisdom Through Questing
◆
The Dark Goddess

INTRODUCTION

Robin Williamson

he goddess of poetry, keeper of the cauldron of inspiration, of birth and rebirth, is in the British Celtic pantheon great mother of all, Ceridwen. She is considered to be the consort of Celu, the unknowable origin and prime cause, and her titles include Nydd, turner of the wheel, and Rhod, the wheel. Her name was transliterated by the Victorian druid Morien O Morgan as Cariadwen, perfect love, but she has the terror face also, as does Kali in Indian cosmology, her aspect being hag of death. She can be thought of as time itself, the ever-rolling stream, the sow that eats her own farrow. But even in this form she remains a life-giver.

◆

HEN WEN

HEN WEN, OLD WHITE, the sow swam out of the sea in the morning of the world. She came ashore in south Wales and shook from her ear a grain of wheat, *gwenydd*, so this part of Wales is called Gwent today and is finest for wheat. Hen Wen swam round to Dyfed and she shook from her ear there a groat of barley and a bee, so you will find honey and good beer in Dyfed to this day (but old ales make young widows in Llangollen, so the saying is, and elsewhere, God knows). Hen Wen swam north and landed in Caernarfon. She climbed the mountain of Snowdon and shook from her ear there a wolf cub and an eagle chick. Men have killed them and their ghosts have infected humans with war. May this curse be lifted. May the wolf and the eagle take again their own freedom and their own power. Hen Wen swam out past Mon (Mon Mam Cymru, Anglesey, mother of Wales). She shook from her ear there into the sea a kitten. It became the whirlpool, Palwg's Cat.

(English version Robin Williamson)

◆

This fragment of Welsh mythology is still current folklore in contemporary south Wales.

Ceridwen's cauldron is in Annwn, under the whirlpool, below the sea, across the sea, over the hill, between one thought and the next, between everything and betwixt every between.

The lore of Annwn is best described in a poem attributed to the bard Taliesin but possibly actually written by Tomas ap Einion in the thirteenth century.

Opposite: *Arthur's ship,* Prydwen *(see overleaf)*

THE SPOILS OF ANNWN

Praise to the Power who orders Highest Heaven
who to the shore of the world extends dominion
fast in the spiral castle Gwair was prisoned
in Caer Siddi
no one before Gwair suffered the like confinement
the chain that bound him was the boundless ocean
among the wealth of the dead his lamentation
and dolorous his song till the day of doom
we went there three times the fill of the ship Prydwen
none returned from spiral castle but seven men
of all that company
none but seven returned from Caer Siddi

am I not worthy of fame and honour in song?
in the four-cornered castle four times spun
who else can say what primal word was spoken?
from the cauldron warmed by the breath of the nine virgins
from the pearl-rimmed cauldron of the Lord of Annwn
that will boil no coward's food nor one foresworn
to these will be brought a death sharp and shining
by the sword that will be left in Lleminawg's right hand
in the gate of coldness horns of light were burning
in that high campaign of the king we were his companions
none returned from the castle of revels but seven men
all others died
none but seven returned from Caer Fedwyd

am I not worthy of fame and song for ever?
in the four-cornered castle in the island of the strong door
where shadows and the darkness meet together
and bright wine brims over in every beaker
three times the fill of Arthur's ship we crossed the waters
none but seven returned from the castle of the rulers
none but seven returned from Caer Rigor

I allow the kings of the story little honour
that beyond the glass castle saw not the prowess of Arthur
six thousand men arrayed along those ramparts
with their watchmen we could scarce confer
three times the fill of Prydwen we went with Arthur
none but seven returned from the castle of treasure
none but seven returned from Caer Colur

little praise to men of little valour
they know neither the day nor its author
of Cwys's birth they know not the hour
nor who from the dales of Defwy was his barrier
they know not the brindled ox nor its halter
nor the seven-score hand-breadths of its collar
ah, when we went with the king, mournful the memory
none but seven returned from Caer Fandwy

men of no courage merit no praise
they know not on what day the ruler arose
nor in what hour the owner was
nor of what kind was his silver-headed beast
ah, when we went with the king, grief of armed men
none but seven returned from Caer Ochren.

(English version by Robin Williamson)

Picture an island fortress which spins, such as the one mentioned later in the 'Voyage of Mael Duinn' (see pages 52–57). The door is circular, the door spins, before the castle door stand the three cranes of denial and churlishness. One croaks, 'Turn back', one urges, 'Venture no further', one shrieks, 'Pass by.' In this Otherworld place of Caer Siddi is found the perfect chair of the bards. But the perfect chair is to be found in this world also, in Abred, and in the world beyond, in Gwynwyd. The chair of the bards is a state of mind.

In bardic philosophy Annwn is not the same as the realm of dreams. Neither is it quite the same concept as the astral plane. It is not necessary to take potions to enter it. Rather, one might say, it enters the heart when the heart is ready. It is not the realm of the dead so much as the realm of the unborn. And the way I see it, faery

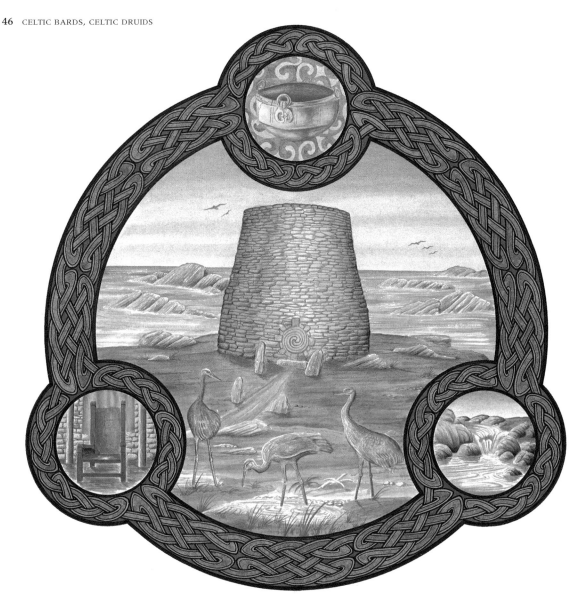

Above: *The whirling castle*

Right: *The triple queen, triple goddess*

is a wee bit different yet again. It is, however, a place of various regions called Caer this and Caer that. The bards were concerned with inspiration.

Ceridwen's cauldron is Annwn. The cauldron is the container, it holds the great brew of as yet unthought wisdom. This is plainly available to anyone who thirsts after it. The cauldron should be understood to hold the nourishment of the soul, containing:

> **The three ever present:**
> Deity, truth, perfection.

These three are ever present in Annwn, ever present in Abred, ever present in Gwynwyd. The Irish concept of the Sidhe resembles the British Annwn. Traditional teachings about Annwn and the Sidhe, or about Celtic philosophy of art in general, are found in stories with the metaphors of battles, raids, voyages and wooings.

THE WOOING OF FINDABAIR

FROECH'S FATHER WAS a king in Ireland. There were many kings and queens of Ireland in those days. Froech's father was a king, but his mother was out of the Sidhe. And his mother's sister was a goddess in her own right, Boand, goddess of the River Boyne. So Froech had power behind him that would make him the finest warrior of Ireland or Scotland while he lived. He did not die old, but it is not the story of his death I am relating but the story of his wooing.

The finest princess in Ireland and the most beautiful was Findabair, daughter of King Ailill and Queen Medh. She fell in love with Froech before she ever saw him, for the mouths of poets were full of his fame. And on the day that Findabair saw him, he saw her with the love that was in her eye. He set his heart to win her.

So Froech went to his mother's sister to ask for bridal gifts out of the Sidhe and with the gifts that he obtained of gold and jewelled weapons, he brought 500 well-armed warriors with dappled horses, white hounds and clothing of crimson, beetle-back blue and snowy white, such that they were a great wonder before the whole world.

With Froech came the three sons of Boand, Froech's cousins, the high harpers of the Sidhe.

This was the host of Froech that set out to the kingdom of Ailill and Medh and to their palace at Cruachu.

The watchman on the walls there saw them coming in the light of day. He ran to Ailill and Medh saying:

> Since first you reigned in Cruachu
> I have kept watch upon your walls
> No such host before has ever approached your fortress
> The breath of their coming is like a wind
> Breathing that wind my head feels soused in wine
> The warrior who leads them performs a feat
> He casts a spear before him
> Seven hounds with silver chains have caught it
> Before it strikes the ground.

The host of Froech reined in before the gates of Cruachu, unbridled the horses, unleashed the hounds. Heralds sang out the true name of Froech and the true names of his company. Ailill and Medh made welcome to them an entire quarter of their palace. They wished to win the help of Froech and his fine warriors, though there was little friendship between Froech's family and their own.

Now the palace of Cruachu was made in seven rows, seven separate quarters about the house from the fire to the wall. Each quarter had a screen of bronze with carved red yew. The palace was made of pine, shingle-roofed. Sixteen windows were in it. A copper shutter for each window. A copper shutter for the skylight. In the middle of the house was the quarter of Ailill and Medh, pillared with copper, set with bronze and girdled with gilded silver. Froech and his company made formal circuit of the palace, from one door to the other. They hung up their weapons and set themselves down.

Ailill said to Froech, 'Let the harpers play for us. The high harpers of the Sidhe.'

Froech asked it of them.

The harp cases were otter-skin, ornamented with virgin leather and with gold and silver. Kid-skin about the harps was white as snow, with dark eyes drawn centrally. Coverings of linen about the strings of the harps was white as swan wings. The harps were covered with gold, silver and white gold in the forms of serpents, birds and hounds.

As the three harpers took up their harps and placed their fingers on the strings, the golden shapes of the animals seemed to move around the chamber, for these harpers were the masters of every music.

Their father, Uaithne, was harper to the Dagda himself, the good father of gods and men. I will tell how the sons of Uaithne got their names.

Uaithne was playing the harp to ease the labour of his wife, Boand. While the first son was born, Uaithne was playing a sorrowful music for the sharpness of the pain Boand had to bear. So the first son was named Goltraigh, which means sorrowful music. At the birth of the second son Uaithne was playing a joyful music, because of the birth of two fine sons. So the second son was named Geantraigh, which means joyful music. When the last son was born, Uaithne played a healing and restful music, so the last son was named Suantraigh, which means music of healing and rest.

These are the three kinds of music in the world and this was the first time they were ever heard in the world.

When the harpers ceased playing, Ailill and Medh said to Froech, 'Indeed, this is the sweetest hour we have ever spent.'

'We have been here three days and three nights together,' was the answer Froech gave back to them.

With that the rulers of Cruachu remembered their duty to their guests. Meat of the red deer was roasted. There was drink of the full glass. In all that time Froech had said no word to Findabair, nor mentioned his wooing to her parents, though it was to court her he had come so far.

On the fourth day's dawn he went down to the river where Findabair would go to bathe.

'Come with me today, love, and leave your parents.' These words Froech said to her, but she said, 'You will win my hand with the consent of my father and mother. Since there is love in my heart for you of all the men in Ireland, take this gold ring.'

The ring she gave him was the royal ring of Cruachu. Froech put it in the pouch that hung from his waist.

Froech went to Ailill and Medh to learn what they would require for their daughter's bride price.

'Three twenties of dark horses
Twelve milk cows, each in calf
And this above all
That you will join us with your company of warriors and your
    harpers
Upon the cattle raid that we will make on Cúailnge.'

'I will pay any price, but I will not make raid on Cúailnge,' said Froech. Angrily, he walked away from them.

Ailill and Medh spoke then into each other's ear.

'The kings of Ireland will think us weak if he takes the girl from us in defiance of our strength.'

'Though we need him sorely as ally with such warriors as he has and with such harpers.'

'It would be better to kill him now before he could carry word away.'

'If it could be so arranged that no dishonour fall on us.'

They went to Froech then, where he sat beside the river, saying, 'We have heard you are a fine swimmer, Froech. Will you not swim for us in the Pool of the Rock of the Rowan Tree?'

'What kind of pool is that?' said Froech.

'God knows, it is the deepest pool in all the river, the darkest and the widest, but certainly we know of nothing dangerous in it. We often swim there ourselves.'

They went to the Pool of the Rock of the Rowan Tree.

Froech took off his clothes and with them his belt and pouch. He left them on the bank and leapt into the black waters.

As he was swimming, Ailill opened Froech's pouch. He found the ring there that Findabair had given him. It was indeed a royal ring of Cruachu. Ailill made haste to throw the ring into deepest part of the pool, for he had it in mind to ask it of Findabair, knowing she could not produce it. Froech, from the corner of his eye, saw the glint of the gold ring through the air. He saw where a salmon in the water snapped at the ring and swallowed it. Froech swam below the water, caught the salmon by the gills and hid the fish in a secret place, unseen among the stones below the far bank.

Froech swam back. He was wading ashore.

Ailill said, 'Will you not bring us a branch of the rowan tree that grows upon the rock in the Pool of the Rock of the Rowan Tree, for these are berries of great virtue as our druids have told us.'

So Froech swam out to the island and brought a branch back to them through the water.

Findabair would say ever after that whatever beautiful things she had seen, the most beautiful was Froech in the water with the rowan branch in his hand.

> 'The white of his skin
> The yellow of his hair
> The blue of his eyes
> The red berries of the rowan branch between his throat and his
>   face.'

Ailill said, 'These rowan berries are more fine and more red than any others in the world. They are indeed a most potent charm, as our druids have informed us. Will you not bring us one branch more, since swimming is to you what walking is to another?'

Froech went back into the pool. As he did, the water dragon that lived below the Island of the Rowan Tree had wakened now. The dragon coiled out below the water and seized him about the waist.

'Throw me a sword,' said Froech.

No one dared for fear of Ailill.

Findabair threw off her clothes

And leapt into the water with a sword

Ailill threw a five-point spear at her

It tangled through two tresses of her hair

Froech caught the spear as he was grappling with the dragon

He threw it back with skill and without vengeance

> For it tore only Ailill's scarlet cloak
> And Ailill's white shirt
> Froech took the sword from Findabair
> And stabbed it into the gills of the water dragon, piercing
>   its brain
> The black water foamed red and seemed to boil with the water
>   dragon's dying
> It was an hour twisting like a spade-cut worm

As Froech was wading to the bank with Findabair's arm about him, it was clear that he was mortally wounded. As he came out of the water, his legs failed under him. He fell into a swoon. They carried Froech to the palace then.

Ailill and Medh spoke then into each other's ear.

'We have done no great deed today.'

'We repent what we have done to Froech.'

'Findabair, however, will have to die.'

'Not because she carried the sword to him, but because she gave him the ring without our knowledge.'

They ordered a healing bath to be prepared for Froech, with fresh bacon and young horseflesh boiled in it, as custom required for nobles. Women washed Froech in the bath, cleansed his wounds and the blood from his hair. He was laid upon a linen-covered bed, a man about to die.

It was then that the people in Cruachu could hear the sound of weeping and of lamentation outside their walls. There were before the gates three fifties of fine women in scarlet and bright green.

Froech, opening his eyes in the whiteness of his face, said, 'These are my mother's people who have come for me.'

The women carried Froech out of Cruachu. They stepped from the palace gates and in that step entered into the world of the Sidhe.

But the very next night as the sun was setting the people of Cruachu saw Froech return. He had no wound upon him now but the full freshness of life and youth.

Ailill and Medh made peace with him. There was feasting, and amid the festivity Froech called one of his servants to him, saying, 'I left a salmon in the rocks beside the waters of the pool. Bring it secretly to me. The ring of Ailill is inside the salmon. I think it will be asked of Findabair tonight.'

Soft soothing draughts and strong drinks were drunk. Little pints of ale and great stammering drams. The riches of Cruachu were displayed and were admired by all.

'Will you not show us the gold ring I gave you?' said Ailill to Findabair. 'Give it to me so that I may show it to the warriors.'

'God knows, I do not have it,' said Findabair. 'I have lost it.'

'Find it,' said Ailill, 'or your soul will leave your body.'

'There is no treasure I would not give for Findabair,' said Froech.

'No treasure you can give will save her life,' said Ailill. 'If she cannot produce the ring, she must die. That is why I demand it.'

'If the ring can be produced,' said Froech, 'swear that Findabair will remain no longer under your protection.'

'I will swear this by the gods my people swear by,' said Ailill.

Froech told his serving boy to give the salmon he had on a platter to Findabair's maid. When the salmon was opened the ring was found.

They gave them a wedding of nine days and nine nights. The last night was better than the first.

Now from that time a good harper can play with the sweetness first learned from the weeping of the women of the Sidhe in lamentation for the wounding of Froech. And the three kinds of music have been known in the world after the harpers' names when they went with Froech in the wooing of Findabair.

From Scottish/Irish Gaelic tradition
(English version by Robin Williamson)

THE VOYAGE OF MAEL DUINN

IT'S SAID AND said truly of Mael Duinn the strong voyager that he thirsted beyond all other thirsts for vengeance on his father's murderer.

As his chief druid directed, he began to build on a day of power a triple-skinned boat. He was to take with him no more than 17 men and these he chose with care. And being advised of the fortunate day on which to sail, it was on that day the boat was launched. But as Mael Duinn and his men were hoisting away to sea, his three foster brothers swam out to join the crew, for they would not be left behind. Thus there were 21 men on board, against the druid's counsel as it befell.

They sailed to the two small islands they were seeking. On each island was a fortress. From each fortress came the sound of revelry. One voice above the others was roaring boastfully, 'It was myself that killed the father of Mael Duinn.'

There was none so ready as Mael Duinn himself to beach his boat of warriors and to give his sword a bloody home in wounds, to give his axe its purpose and its skill. But a great wind arose. It drove the boat before it far and far into the wild of the deep sea. Striving against that wind, their strength was spent. They surrendered the craft to the wind and the waves of God.

This was the beginning of the great voyage of Mael Duinn and the account of the islands that they passed, seeking ever homeward to Erin, as the bards relate.

They sailed:
    To an island of ants
        Each ant was large as a foal
    To an island of birds
        That were also of great size
    To an island of a fierce and horse-like beast
        Whose feet were sharp-taloned
        Like a hound's claws
    To an island of ever-racing horses
    To an island where the waves were casting salmon
        Through the opening of a stone into a house
    To an island of trees where a cut branch grew three apples
        Each apple fed them all for 40 nights
    To an island of a beast which could turn inside its skin
        And also it could turn its skin about
    To a blood-wet island full of fierce horse-like beasts
        That tore the flesh from one another's flanks
    To an island of fiery swine that slept in caves
        That fed on the golden fruit of apple trees
        That fed on the golden fruit of apple trees.

The next island that they came to they were blown ashore. It was a small and rocky island between the seas. They stumbled up the grey beach to the house that was built there between the boulders. It was a small house made of stone. Silent and deserted it was, yet filled with every kind of priceless treasure. Gold ornaments, mirrors of silver, strings of jewels adorned its walls within. Rich gems of red and green and purple, rubies like eggs that might hatch serpents, agates like small shields in dark green and blue, silver armbands like the caw a high bard wears, chains and torques of gold. There was a table laid with every kind of food and flagons of wine.

In the middle of the house by the far wall stood four pillars of grey stone. There was a little cat that was leaping from one pillar to another. All night long as they were eating, drinking and taking their rest the little cat leapt backwards and forwards without cease upon the heads of the four pillars. In the morning they made ready to return to the boat. The last man out of the door was one of Mael Duinn's foster brothers. He reached out as he passed and lifted a string of jewels from the wall. The little cat leapt from the pillars towards him. And in that leap it became an arrow and which passed into the body of Mael Duinn's foster brother and out at the small of his back. His body as it fell withered into grey ashes which blew away, as they watched, among the grey stones. Among the grey stones.

They sailed:
    To an island of blackness and whiteness
        Dividing it across was a wall of brass
        Black sheep were on one side
        White on the other
        The colour changed of any that leapt across.

They sailed:
    To another land of halves
        An island of giant kine and giant swine
        Between them was running a river of fire
    To an island of a giant miller's mill
        Where that part of the world's grain is ground
        The part a man begrudges to another
    To an island full of black-robed mourners
        Making lament with lamentation
        And there fell to lamenting also
        Mael Duinn's second foster brother
        From his grief they could not rouse him
        They left him there
        They left him there.

They sailed:
    To an isle cut in four with fences
        One gold, one silver, one brass, one crystal
        Dividing kings from queens
        From warriors from maidens
    To an island fortress with a bridge of glass
        But had the power to bar all crossing
        And there a radiant maiden rebuffed the voyagers thrice
        Then straightway made them welcome each by name
        Saying their coming there had been long foretold

The crewmen tried to woo her for Mael Duinn
She said she would make answer on the morn
But when they woke they were again from land
But when they woke they were again from land.

They sailed:
  To an island of shouting birds
  To an island of birds and a saint
      Who wore for garment only his long hair
      Who had come there stood on one turf of his native land
      Which God increased a foot's width
      And by one tree each year
      The birds were his own children
      And his kin
      And there they were awaiting the world's doom
      They would be fed by angels until that time
      The saint foretold of Mael Duinn's journey's end
      That all would reach their home
      Save one man more
      Save one man more.

They sailed:
  To an island with a strange fountain
      Fridays and Wednesdays it ran whey and water
      Sundays milk, feast days ale and wine.

They sailed:
  To an island of a giant smithy
      Where hammering of metal as loud as thunder sounded
      Where black smoke hung in clouds to the horizon.

They sailed:
  Across a sea as clear as clear glass
      And then across a sea half clear like a cloud
      Where in the deeps they saw a beast in a giant tree
      Devour the largest ox in a guarded herd.

They sailed close by the shores of a large island of many towns. Thousands thronged down along the shore peering towards them. Suddenly they all began to shout and scream at once with every sign of extreme fear and terror. 'It is them! It is them!' they were screaming as Mael Duinn and his men were blown by the wind, as ever, away. As ever away.

They sailed:
  To an isle with an arch of water over it
      With salmon swimming up and swimming down.

They could see now looming over the horizon what appeared to be a tower of silver. As they were blown towards it, they could see that it was square, bright-shining and featureless, the top so high it vanished among the clouds. As they sailed near, it seemed that time slowed beneath the height of this vast and lowering wall of metal, their own features staring back at them, so close they were passing. All at once, a great net of silver, shimmering and sparkling, splashed far beyond them

The pigs and the magical apple tree

into the sea. It was as suddenly whisked back into the heights of the tower. A loud voice called out in words they could not understand.

They found themselves being blown in towards a land beyond the tower of silver and as they approached it they could see to their amazement that it was a vast city built upon a pillar of bronze. The pillar rose straight out of the sea and in the pillar's base there was a door. The boat seemed to moor itself against the landing stage beside that door. The door opened.

Mael Duinn and his crew were welcomed into that city by the finest woman any of them had ever seen and with her was a company of women, many hundreds, all young, all beautiful. The queen of these women took Mael Duinn by the hand and led him in the steps of a dance. It seemed to them all, as they remembered it later, as if they were dancing for 100 years. The music, the song seemed to say, 'Stay with us for ever and avoid old age and hardships.' Who would not stay in the land of women, the land of joy, the land of the ever young?

Mael Duinn's heart was still hot with the fire of vengeance. He could not forget the task he had set himself. He ordered a return to the ship.

But the queen threw after them a ball of wool which stuck to Mael Duinn's hand. She pulled the boat back as easy as the tide pulls. Many times then they would try to sail away, by night or in the dark before the dawn. But every time she would pull them back. Until at last one brave crewman leapt up and caught the ball of wool. Laying his wrist against the gunwale, he roared to Mael Duinn to strike off his hand.

They sailed:
>   To the island of the berries of slumber
>   To the isle of the hermit and the ancient eagle
>   Where was a pool whose waters cured all ills
>   To the island of laughter where they left to his laughter
>   Mael Duinn's last foster brother
>   Mael Duinn's last foster brother.

They sailed:
>   To an isle with spinning walls of fire
>   Where as the doorway passed they could see within
>   Fine handsome people clad in kingly colours
>   Give ear to the harp with gold cups in their hands.

They sailed to the island of the monk of Torach. This monk had robbed his own church. He had made off in a coracle with his golden plunder in a bag beside him. But just as he was sure of his escape, a voice out of the air advised him to cast everything he had stolen into the deep. The waves of the sea guided him to the island, where he had lived ever since, and in the solitude of his penance angels fed him each morning with food from paradise.

This man who had so sinned and who had been so forgiven gave Mael Duinn the secret that would end his endless wanderings at the mercy of that ceaseless wind. 'You must forgive, in the heart of your heart, your father's murderer'. These were the words the monk of Torach said to him. 'If you persist in such a quest for vengeance, you will never be permitted to return to your own land.'

Mael Duinn paid heed to what the wise man said and let his anger

fall away from him. As he did, there came winging out of the west a
falcon in every way like the falcons of Erin. It hovered before the boat.
Mael Duinn and his men steered as it guided them. It flew before them,
a faithful navigator, until it led them safe at last to their own harbour.

From Scottish/Irish Gaelic tradition
(English version by Robin Williamson)

◆

CULHWCH AND OLWEN

THE MOTHER OF Culhwch, a beautiful but temperamental lady, became unsettled in her wits during her pregnancy, strayed from civilized places and, returning to her senses near her time, found herself among a herd of pigs. She gave birth to her son in fright at that. The swineherd took the boy to court. That's how Culhwch got his name. It means Pig Run. But he was a king's son, and a cousin to Arthur himself. He was fostered, as was the custom, to a high-born family.

His mother, Goleuddydd, now become mortally ill. She required her royal husband to promise that he would never marry again until he would see a two-headed briar growing on her grave. Secretly, she had requested her old teacher to trim the grave to the ground every year. Goleuddydd died. The king went every morning to look at her grave to see if anything was growing there. At the end of the seventh year, Goleuddydd's old teacher forgot to trim the grave. In the spring thereafter, the king found a briar growing and asked his counsellors to advise him in the choice of a new wife.

'How about the wife of King Doged?' was the word he was given. So they made war on King Doged, killed him and carried his widow and daughter back with them. They took possession of King Doged's land also, and very good land it was.

Now Doged's royal widow was nothing if not adaptable. What seemed to bother her most was that the man who had carried her off so vigorously appeared to have no children. Finally, she inquired privily of an old woman concerning this, saying, 'Sad it is to be wedded to an infertile man.'

'Neither stars nor portents deny him children,' said the hag. 'He shall have children, and by you, I prophesy, my lady, God bless your generosity. Grieve no longer, God reward you, for he has one son.'

That night the lady asked her husband why he had concealed his son from her. 'I will conceal him from you no longer,' said the king. He sent messengers to bring Culhwch back to court.

At a quiet moment soon after, Culhwch's stepmother suggested to him that her daughter would make a wonderful wife for any nobleman.

'I do not wish to marry yet,' said Culhwch.

'I put a curse on you then,' said his stepmother. 'Your flesh shall never touch the flesh of a woman till you get Olwen, daughter of Ysbaddaden, King of all Giants.'

Culhwch blushed at that. Passionate love and desire for Olwen possessed him, though he had never seen her. He blushed often thereafter. One day his father asked him why.

'My stepmother has put a curse on me that my flesh will never touch the flesh of a woman till I get Olwen, daughter of Ysbaddaden, King of all Giants.'

'That's easy for you to achieve, my son. Go to King Arthur, your cousin. Ask him to trim your hair, as a cousinly act of affection, and while he is about it ask that he accomplish this quest for you. He will not fail you.

Culhwch rode off on a young grey steed
of fiery eye, of graceful pace
gold, not leather, about its head

gold, not leather, its saddle was
and Culhwch bore two silver spears
his sword in hand an arm's length
it would wound the wind and swifter drop
than drops the wettest dew of June
on Culhwch's hip, gold-hilted
a gold-edged sword with a gold cross on it
many jewelled as the midnight sky
moon white its ivory grip
by Culhwch there ran two dappled hounds
red gold collars from shoulder to ear
the dog on the left would leap to the right
the dog on the right would leap to the left
like two wild birds they sported round him
the four hoofs of Culhwch's steed
would hurl four clods above Culhwch's head
like four of summer's swooping swallows
a purple, four-cornered cloak he wore
a red gold apple at every corner
each apple worth a hundred cows
the gold in his soft boots and lacings
from the knob of his knee to the nail of his toe
300 cows would hardly buy
so easily the steed moved under him
no curl of Culhwch's hair was stirred
nor even the least tip of one hair
so Culhwch came riding to Arthur's gate.

'Is there a gatekeeper?'

'There is, and may you not keep your head on your shoulders for asking such a question,' came the churlish reply from behind closed doors. 'I am gatekeeper to Arthur every first of January and my sub-ordinates for the rest of the year are Huandaw, Gogigwr, Llaesgenym and Penpingion, who hops on his head to save his feet, never standing nor lying down, but like a rolling stone on the floor of Arthur's court.'

'Open the gate,' said Culhwch.

'I will not,' said the gatekeeper.

'Why will you not?' said Culhwch.

'Knife has gone into meat, drink into drinking horn, there is already a great crowd in the court of Arthur. No one may enter but the son of a king or a man of skill who comes with his craft. You'll get food for your dogs, grain for your horse. You'll get peppered chops and brimming beakers of wine. You'll get enough for 50 in the hostel down the road where strangers who have no right to insist on Arthur's hospitality are accommodated. You'll be just as well off there as Arthur is in his own court, I assure you. You'll get songs to entertain you and a woman to sleep with you, and tomorrow when the gates are opened to permit the exit of the thronging crowds who have descended on us today, they shall be opened to you first of all. And tomorrow, you can seat yourself anywhere you may choose in Arthur's hall.'

'None of this will do,' said Culhwch. 'If you open the door now, well and good. If not, I will voice an ill report of your lord and yourself throughout the land. Further, I will shout three shouts at this gate that will be heard as clearly southerly on the moors of Cornwall, northerly on the shores of the Scots north and on the Accursed Ridge in Ireland.

All pregnant women in the court will miscarry, and all other women here, from the time they hear these shouts, will never conceive at all.'

'Whatever uproar you may raise for the privileges of Arthur's court, you shall not enter,' said the gatekeeper, adding hastily, 'not until I speak to Arthur first.'

The gatekeeper Glewlwyd strode off and flung open the door of Arthur's feasting hall. 'What news from the gate?' asked the king in some surprise. Glewlwyd drew himself up to his full height and, in the grand manner of Taliesin, he proclaimed:

'Two parts of my life have gone
and two parts of your own
I have been in Caer Se and Caer Asse
in Sach and Salach
in Lotor and Fotor
and Greater and Lesser India
I have been in the battle of the two Ynyrs
when twelve hostages were taken from Llychlyn
I have been once in Europe
I have been once in Africa, Corsica likewise
in Caer Brythwch and Brythach and Nerthach
I have been at hand when you killed the entire army
of Gleis son of Merin
and when you killed Black Mil son of Dugum
I have been right beside you when you conquered Greece
    altogether
I have been, I declare, in Caer Oeth and Anoeth
the dark prisons under stone
and in Caer Nevenhyr of the nine natures.'

'Yes, yes,' snapped Arthur, 'but what news from the gate?'

'Fair lords we encountered in performance of these exploits,' continued Glewlwyd, not a whit abashed, 'but I never saw a man as noble as he I have left standing at the gate in the rain.'

'If you came to me walking, go back running,' roared Arthur. 'Bring this man in. Servants, bring him a gold cup and keep it full. Give him some chops.'

It was the custom to dismount at the gate, but Culhwch, when the door was opened to him, rode straight into the hall, dogs and all. 'Greetings, Lord of Kings in this island,' he said. 'May the low part of your house be no worse than the high. May this greeting reach equally your fighting men, your companions and your warlords. May no one here be deprived of this my greeting. May your fame, Arthur, resound throughout Britain.'

'Greetings to you also, chieftain. Sit here by me among the warriors. You shall have the privileges of a prince when you are here.'

'I did not come here for recognition, but to ask one boon of you.'

'You shall have whatever
your tongue can utter
while the wind blows with the wetness of rain
and the full extent
of your mind's invention
while sun lifts day to the last ebb of land
except my sword, my shield, my spear
or my wife Gwenhwyfar.'

'I ask first that my hair be trimmed.'

'You shall get that,' said Arthur, and taking a golden comb and silver-handled scissors, he commenced to comb and trim the hair of Culhwch. But as he was about this he felt his heart warm to Culhwch, and he said to him, 'I know in my heart we must be kindred. Tell me who you are.'

'I will. I am Culhwch son of Cilydd son of Celyddon Wledig, and of Goleuddydd my mother.'

'Then,' said Arthur, 'you are my cousin. Claim what you will of me.'

'Help me to win the hand of Olwen daughter of Ysbaddaden, King of all Giants.'

Culhwch invoked this help with a highly skilled bardic incantation on the names of Arthur's assembled warriors, not one of whom he had met before. He expanded with wit and delightful language upon their fame and prowess, till an hour was as a moment. And Culhwch invoked this help in the names of the greatest ladies of Arthur's court after Gwenhwyfar, with their full poetic titles, powers and beauties. And this incantation he performed with resonance, with good humour and with a melodious tongue.

'Well,' said Arthur finally, 'I never heard of Olwen or of this King of Giants, but I will send messengers to seek news of her. It may take some time to find her.'

'I will give you from tonight until a year from tomorrow night.'

At the end of a year, no news had been obtained. Culhwch became disgruntled and threatened to leave, reciting satires on Arthur's court throughout the island.

But Arthur's great warrior Cei made this placation to him, saying, 'Do not be so hasty. Journey with us till you are satisfied that this maiden Olwen is not to be found in the world. Or until we find her.'

These were the powers of Cei:

He could retain in sea deep
one breath nine days and nights
beyond herbs or healer's skill
any wound he would inflict
shadow light Cei could step
or seem tree tall at will.

Whatever Cei gripped would remain dry even in pelting rain from the heat of his hand, and in falling snow the snap of his fingers could kindle fire.

With them came Bedwyr, who never shied from any exploit in which Cei was engaged. He was the most beautiful man in Britain after Arthur and Drych, son of Cibddar.

If he fought one-handed
three armed men could not best him
he gave with one spear thrust
one death and nine defences.

With them went Cynddilyd the Guide, to whom all lands were as his own land, and Gwrhyr the Interpreter, to whom all tongues were as his own tongue, and Gwalchmai, who accomplished every quest he undertook, and Menw, who was a master of every kind of magic.

These heroes set forth upon their journey and they journeyed till they reached a huge plain, where grazed a flock of sheep as numerous as the white waves of the sea. And there, on a mound, sat a sheep-dog as big as a cart-horse and a shepherd who was not undersized himself.

This was the shepherd's usual habit
to let no warrior pass unharmed
this was the strength of the shepherd's breath
to burn branches and brushwood down.

'Go and speak to him,' said Cei to Gwrhyr. 'I promised only to go as far as you do,' said Gwrhyr to Cei. 'Fear not,' said Menw. 'I will put an enchantment on the dog so that he cannot harm us.' With some caution they went forward and gave the shepherd a most courteous greeting.

'How are you, noble shepherd?'

'Apart from my wife, no wound annoys me,' rumbled the shepherd.

'Whose sheep are these?'

'These are the sheep of Ysbaddaden, King of all Giants. And whose sheep are you?'

'We are messengers from Arthur, High King of Britain, sent to seek the hand of Olwen.' And they told him their names.

'More fools you,' laughed the shepherd,, 'No cock upon that quest has ever lived to crow about it.'

Culhwch offered the shepherd, as a token of their goodwill, his gold armband, which the shepherd with a guffaw squeezed on to the little finger of his glove and, still laughing, strode off home to his wife.

'Where did you get that ring, husband?'

'Off a corpse the tide washed in.'

But the wife was not satisfied with such a reply, and she was not long in wheedling out the whole story. She knew then that Culhwch was her nephew, for she was the sister of Goleuddydd. And she determined to see him for herself.

As she ran joyfully towards these knights of Arthur with her arms outstretched to hug them, Cei, the first she came to grips with, had the presence of mind to snatch up a log between himself and her. And such was the ardour of her embrace, that she made sap run from the log like whey from cheese. 'God knows,' muttered Cei:

'But for this log
that hug, you hag,
I would have squeezed the last squawk
out of my bag.'

Unoffendable, Culhwch's auntie invited them home for a meal. And after it, as they were conversing of this and that, she opened a cupboard by the fire and a beautiful yellow-haired boy stepped out.

'What a pity to hide such a boy,' said Gwrhyr.

'The only one I have left,' said the shepherd's wife. 'Ysbaddaden has killed 23 of my sons, and my only hope is to keep this one out of his sight.'

'Let him remain with me,' said Cei. 'And he will not be slain unless I am. Help us to win Olwen for Culhwch, your nephew.'

'For God's sake, venture no further with that. Ysbaddaden does not know you are here. Go home while you can.'

Olwen

But insisting they would not leave until they had seen the maiden, they at length found out that the shepherd's wife was Olwen's old nurse and that Olwen was in the habit of visiting her every Saturday to wash her hair. They gave their word of honour that they would do Olwen no harm. The shepherd's wife at last agreed to arrange their meeting with her.

> Olwen's dress was flame red
> red gold and garnets about her neck
> yellow her hair as yellow broom
> sea foam no whiter than her white skin
> her fingers white as water flowers
> her eyes bird bright, her swan white breasts
> her cheek's blush like foxglove flowers
> filled any man with love of her.

Four white clovers sprang in her footsteps where she walked. It was for this she was called by the name Olwen. It means White Track.

As soon as Culhwch saw her, he said to her, 'Maiden, it is you and you alone I love. Bind your life with mine, my darling, and come away with me.'

'Speak no more such words,' whispered Olwen. 'I cannot go away with you. It is the nature of my father's fate that he will die if I ever marry. But if you go to my father and ask for my hand in marriage, I will give you this advice. Promise to procure for him whatever he will ask of you. Any hesitation will be certain death to you all. It is also certain that my father will now know you are here. You must go to him.'

They went with her to the fortress of Ysbaddaden and entered after her the hugest gate they had ever seen and followed her into the hall of the King of all Giants and found him asleep and snoring.

'Greetings, Ysbaddaden, King of all Giants.'

'Who speaks?' grunted Ysbaddaden. 'Where are my useless gate-keepers?'

'We are messengers from Arthur seeking the hand of your daughter, Olwen, for Culhwch, son of Cilydd.'

'Why do I bother paying servants? Why do I bother feeding attendants? Prop up the forks under my eyelids so I can see my future son-in-law.'

So they propped great pitchforks up under the giant's eyelids. The giant scowled at them with his stone-grey eyes.

'Come back tomorrow,' he thundered.

They turned to leave, but as they did, Ysbaddaden picked up the nearest of the three poisoned spears he had propped beside him and he hurled it at them. Bedwyr caught it and hurled it back. It pierced Ysbaddaden through the kneecap, and Ysbaddaden said:

> 'Uncivil pest of a son-in-law this
> ever the worse I shall walk up hill
> the poison spear stings like a wasp sting
> damn the smith that forged it
> and damn his anvil.'

The following day they came to him again. 'Ysbaddaden, King of All Giants, we seek your daughter's hand for Culhwch.'

Opposite: *Ysbaddaden*

'Her four great-grandmothers and her four great-grandfathers are yet alive. I must ask their counsel. Come back tomorrow.'

They turned to leave, but as they did, Ysbaddaden snatched up the second of his poisoned spears and he hurled it at them. Menw caught it and hurled it back. It pierced Ysbaddaden in the hollow below his ribs.

'A double damned ungentlemanly son-in-law this
like the bite of a horse leech
the cold iron cuts me
damn the forge that heated it
every time I walk up hill
I'll have heartburn, gut ache
and a wee bit of indigestion even.'

The third day they came to him again. 'Throw no more spears at us, Ysbaddaden. Seek not your own death before your time.'

'Where are my servants? Prop up my eyelids with the forks again.' They did that, and as they did Ysbaddaden snatched up the third poisoned spear and hurled it at them. Culhwch caught it and hurled it back. It pierced Ysbaddaden in the eyeball.

'A bloody cur of a son-in-law if you ask me
the poison iron bites me like a mad dog
against the wind my eyes will water
as long as I live my sight will be a mite less than perfect
severe headaches will plague me
and giddiness at new moon.'

The next day they came to him again. Ysbaddaden said to them, 'Come forward to me, the one who seeks my daughter.' Culhwch came forward. 'I will set you tasks, and when you have accomplished them you will be married to my daughter. Out of the wood that surrounds my fortress, a field must be cleared and the brush burnt and ploughed under. That field must be sowed with grain. It must sprout, ripen, be harvested and be ground into corn, and all this must be accomplished by the dew fall of tomorrow's first light. This will be the making of your wedding feast.

'This will be easy for me, though you might think it difficult,' said Culhwch.

Ysbaddaden next expounded an extraordinary rigmarole of completely impossible requirements, which included no fewer than nine of the thirteen treasures of Britain and the birds of Rhiannon. One requirement could not be fulfilled without the completion of the next, and each required the help of some ancient hero whose help seemed impossible to obtain. In this way Ysbaddaden thought to preserve his life, which would be forfeit if Olwen were ever to marry.

But whatever Ysbaddaden asked, Culhwch agreed to perform, saying, 'This will be easy for me, though you might think it difficult.' Finally Ysbaddaden set the hardest task of all. It was that his hair and beard must be trimmed. No more than Culhwch had asked Arthur, you would think. But no scissors, razor or comb in the world would serve except those that hung between the ears of the giant boar Twrch Trwyth. No one could hunt him but Mabon, son of Modron, the greatest of all huntsmen, stolen when he was three days old from between his mother and the wall, prisoned and lost beyond the reach of love or war.

But Culhwch said, 'That will be easy for me, though you might think that is difficult. And with the help of my kinsman Arthur, I will perform all these tasks.'

They returned to Arthur and with all his company they set out to seek Mabon. They went first to the oldest bird of the forest, the Blackbird of Cilgwri, and Gwrhyr the Interpreter of Tongues addressed him:

'Wise and ancient Bird of the Forest
Bird of the Forest, know you aught of Mabon
Mabon who, when he was three days old, was stolen
stolen from between his mother and the wall?'

And the bird replied:
'In my first feather I first came here
to these green woods where I make my home
to keep the sharp edge on my beak
I found an old smith's anvil for a sharpening stone
now only this scrap of the anvil remains
though no hammer beat it but my beak alone
but in all these years past and gone
I never heard of this man Mabon
But if anyone would know, it would be the Stag of Rhedynfre.'

So they set out to find him, and Gwrhyr addressed him, saying:

'Wise and ancient Stag of the Mountain
Stag of the Mountain, know you aught of Mabon
Mabon who, when he was three days old, was stolen
stolen from between his mother and the wall?'

And the Stag replied:
'A greenhorn buck I first came here
when this ancient oak was a verdant sprout
I have seen it stretch forth 100 boughs
I have seen it wither, I have seen it rot
till only this stump of the oak remains
and that no bigger than my forefoot
but in all these years, past and gone
I never heard of this man Mabon.
But if anyone would know, it would be the Eagle of
    Gwernabwy.'

They went to the eagle, and Gwrhyr addressed him:
'Wise and ancient Eagle of Kingdoms
Eagle of Kingdoms, know you aught of Mabon
Mabon who, when he was three days old was stolen
stolen from between his mother and the wall?'

And the eagle replied:
'Long and since when I first came here
this crag of mine was a crag indeed
every evening I could peck at the stars
as they whirled in their fires about my head
my talons have worn the rock away
to this rump of a boulder on which I perch

but in all those years past and gone
I never heard of this man Mabon.
But if anyone would know, it would be the Salmon of
    Llyn Llyw.'

So they went to the salmon, and Gwyrhyr addressed him:
'Wise and ancient Salmon of Wisdom
Salmon of Wisdom, know you aught of Mabon
Mabon who when he was three days old, was stolen
stolen from between his mother and the wall?'

And the salmon replied:
'I will tell you as much as I know
and that is more than any other can tell
I have swum east, I have swum west
I have swum in the deeps below Gloucester's walls
and there heard sighing and lamentation
as never was heard since the world began
that you may believe that this was Mabon
I will ferry you straight to the dark prison.'

Cei and Gwrhyr rode astride the salmon's shoulders until they reached the walls of the dark prison at Caer Loyw, which is now called Gloucester. They called to the prisoner within, 'Who are you here confined that cries and laments so sadly?' And learning that this indeed was Mabon, they rescued him by force of Arthur's soldiers and continued on their quest with him. They accomplished every difficult feat that had been set them by Ysbaddaden in procuring the dogs, the leashes and all else necessary to hunt the giant boar Twrch Trwyth.

They sent Menw of the Many Skills into Ireland to ascertain the whereabouts of Twrch Trwyth. It was not hard to get news of him; he had already laid waste one third of Ireland. Menw, learning that Twrch Trwyth had made a lair for himself upon the Accursed Ridge, turned himself into a great hawk. He hoped to make off with the razor, comb or scissors that hung between the ears of Twrch Trwyth, the only implements that could be used to trim the hair and beard of Ysbaddaden.

As he sped towards the Accursed Ridge he could see against the skyline the hump of Twrch Trwyth's back from many miles' distance. Some say Twrch Trwyth had been a king turned by God into a boar for his sins, some say he was a kind of god or demon himself, but he was bigger than seven horses, more ferocious than seven lions, his lust for destruction grew seven times the greater with every seven men he destroyed. Seven of his young dwelt with him.

As Menw fluttered swiftly the length of the enormous, black-bristled spine, there gleamed before him the great comb, the razor and scissors, silver bright and long as spears. Between the two huge ears that quivered to the east and west of him like two black sails, he was able to grasp no more than one hair. Even so poison from the boar spattered upon him. He was marked by it till the day of his death.

Arthur assembled the warriors of the three islands of Britain and of their adjacent islands and of France, Brittany, Normandy and the Land of Summer. It was with these multitudes that Arthur came to the Accursed Ridge. Whatever approach the Irish armies made in a day and a night, another fifth of Ireland was destroyed by Twrch Trwyth. In a new day, Arthur's armies marched towards Twrch Trwyth in their turn, and every step of their advance was death and misery to them.

Arthur sent Gwrhyr the Interpreter to parley with Twrch Trwyth, and Twrch Trwyth gave him this reply: 'By the name of the God who caused me this grief, I have nothing to say to Arthur. He will never get the razor, comb or scissors while I am alive. Tomorrow I will swim to Britain, and there I will wreak such destruction as will give you cause to rue that ever you hunted me out.'

And so it was. The next day Twrch Trwyth swam ashore with his young in west Wales. Throughout the length and breadth of Britain, Mabon, the son of Modron, the greatest huntsman in the world, hunted him with the two enchanted dogs that had been obtained for him by the questing of Arthur's knights. And in that hunting, Twrch Trwyth slew many of Arthur's greatest heroes. Finally, Mabon hunted Twrch Trwyth to the shores of the Severn, and there Arthur and the champions of Britain fell upon him, and together they managed to drive him into deep waters. Mabon snatched the razor from between his ears. Cyledyr the Wild carried off the scissors. But before anyone could grasp the comb, Twrch Trwyth was able to regain his footing and reaching land, neither horse nor hound could keep up with him until he reached Cornwall.

Whatever hardship Arthur and his warriors had had from Twrch Trwyth before was but play to the taking of the comb. But take it they did at last. They drove Twrch Trwyth into the sea. And where he went from that time is not known.

Arthur then obtained and performed all that Ysbaddaden had set them. Even the blood of the Tar Black Witch daughter of the Ice White Witch from the Valley of Grief in the north of Hell, Arthur obtained in the fulfilment of his promise to Culhwch.

So it was that they returned to the court of Ysbaddaden. They clipped and shaved Ysbaddaden. They shaved his flesh and skin to the bone, and the two ears from his head. 'Have you been shaved, Ysbaddaden?' asked Culhwch. 'Is your daughter Olwen now mine?'

'I have been shaved,' said Ysbaddaden, 'Olwen is now yours. Though but for Arthur, you never would have gained her. Now is the time to end my life.'

They cut the head from Ysbaddaden then. That night Culhwch slept with Olwen. As long as he lived, she was his only wife.

From Welsh tradition (English version by Robin Williamson)

THE SONG OF MABON

We've been rambling all the night
and some part of this day
back we are returned again
to bring you a branch of may

a story to be told when journeys are broken
by fall of night or by first light of day
a secret to be spoken when turnings are taken
by spring's first flower or by first shower of snow
a song to be whispered to ears that will listen
for love of the red rose
for love of the white rose

o the may, the bonny may
the branch we bear so green
rise up rise up you maidens all
out of your rosy dream

it is of the royal road
by may day and midwinter and summer's end
it is of the boundaries of the world
and the other world
it is of the choice made when no choice is given
and of the weight of the horned mask on the face
by the gallows, the cradle and the bridal feast
I trace now my own features in the stone

red blood runs
from the mouth of the white deer
the red-eared hounds
are white as the snow is white

frost white blossom, flower fire
I have craved safe avenues
and well-frequented love
some armament to raise against the cold
some grave, some mirror
not to be seen beyond

red blood runs
from the mouth of the white deer
the red-eared hounds
are white

lady, I am a figment
I am a blight, I am an ember
one mirror for all memory
that steals what is true
and a voice buried in my heart is crying
I am the risk and purchase of the world
carry me with you.

Robin Williamson

◆

THE PALACE OF CRYSTAL

Introduction *by R. J. Stewart*

Each Celtic realm preserves its own ideas of the Otherworld in oral tradition, uniquely coloured by the land and culture. Thus there are many differences between Breton, Welsh, Irish, Scottish, Manx, Cornish and European Celtic traditions. Nevertheless, we find certain enduring themes that are handed down from the pagan era, the time of the druids, often preserved by bards, poets and travelling singers.

'The Palace of Crystal' was collected in the nineteenth century, yet includes material that we find in bardic philosophy from earlier times and from Celtic paganism of the pre-Christian era. Despite some Christian moralizing, the story is of an Otherworld journey, of tests and of the connection between the spiritual life and the human outer life. The tale was noted from a traditional story-teller, as handed down by word of mouth through the generations.

The first half involves, like many fairy-tales, some arrogant brothers who fail in their quest to find their sister, who has married a mysterious shining young man and travelled with him to the Palace of Crystal. The second half, also like many fairy-tales, concerns the youngest brother, Yvon, whom the family has always mocked and scorned. He gets further than anyone, yet fails the ultimate test of the Underworld.

The two halves of the tale are different in tone. In the first, the arrogant brothers meet a hag, a traditional embodiment of the ancient goddess of death and regeneration. They also meet her giant son, who initially seeks to eat them. This giant burns like the sun and works his fire-magic to take them part of the way to the Palace of Crystal. But they fail when he leaves them and they return home.

In the second part Yvon gains entry to the palace after many trials and tests, and finds that the laws of this shining realm are often the reverse of human laws. Both Yvon and his sister long to know where her husband, the handsome shining stranger, goes each day. Yvon is told that he can accompany him, but that he must talk to no one and touch nothing on the journey. This he fails to do and so is forbidden the last of three stages, the entry to the Underworld. He is sent back and finds that centuries have passed and his family is extinct. So he prays to die, seeking to return to the palace in death.

The three parts of the tale relate how a human may pass through the three realms of being, a typically Celtic/druidic theme. The first realm is reached directly from the human world, and is indeed part of it, for it is the realm of living nature. Its components are the vast forest, the Goddess of the land and the giant vitality of her child, the physical sun which both destroys and sustains.

The second realm is that of the inner powers behind living nature, in which the mysteries of consciousness, of polarity, are

learned. This is a typical tale of the quest for reality, for magical power, for spiritual enlightenment. The embodiment of light is the shining stranger, who is a sun god and an initiator into the mysteries of inner truth, where polarities, laws, actions, thoughts and feeling are all reversed. To reach this realm is hard enough, but to keep its laws is even harder.

The third realm is that of the ancient mysteries, for it is where the sun goes when it is unseen. Traditionally, this is the deepest Underworld, and although it is rationalized as '*l'enfer*', or Hell, the story makes clear that this is the greatest mystery, one which Yvon fails. The gate of Hell is featured in a number of Breton tales, and the terrifying noises mentioned in the story are only the first level, often involving the conquest of fear. Beyond the frightening sounds of many voices is the deeper Underworld, where the sun regenerates out of darkness. Yvon, however, has conquered fear in his earlier adventures and is forbidden entry because he failed to keep the laws of the second realm.

Finally, we learn that the second realm, the Palace of Crystal, where all things are reversed, is also the world of the afterlife. First, Yvon is told this by his brother-in-law, and when he dies at the end of the tale he returns there.

Typical druidic elements in the tale are as follows:
1 The nature powers, the test of the forest, the goddess and the giant.
2 The three realms (though allocation or description of these realms varies frequently).
3 The importance of imagination and fear on the quest
4 The significance of polarity reversals.
5 The rule of obedience to inner laws.
6 The mystery of spiritual regeneration, embodied by the sun sinking into the earth, passing through the Underworld and returning whole.

We might add some other elements from Celtic tradition: the significance of horses in the Otherworld, the entrance through a dolmen (megalithic chamber), the crossing of a great black lake or sea to reach the Otherworld, and the paradox of time (found in many tales where a short stay in the faery realm equals centuries in the human world). Of speculative interest is the way in which Yvon breaks his vow of silence and of not touching anything. He sees two trees fighting bitterly, and separates them with his staff. This tree battle is a central druidic/bardic theme, and it seems likely that the episode is a compact rationalization of a longer sequence. Druids had the right to separate combatants with a staff in ancient Ireland and Wales. We are then told that the trees were a quarrelling couple doing penance, so Yvon clearly has some power by this stage, for he frees them from their eternal struggle. Yet this is his undoing, and for breaking the laws of the realm, he cannot remain or travel further with his radiant brother-in-law.

MacRoth/MogRuith, the flying druid, embodiment of a Celtic sun god

A POOR PEASANT couple had seven children, six sons and a daughter. The two youngest, the boy Yvon and his sister Yvonne, were said to be fools, and their older brothers tormented them ceaselessly. As a result, Yvonne never smiled, but sadly went each day to the wild heath to look after the cows and sheep. All she had was a piece of rough bread and some water, and she had to stay out on the heath until sunset.

One morning, as she led her herd to the wild heath, she met a handsome young man, out in the wilderness. He shone so brightly that he seemed like the sun itself, and he came right up to her and said, 'Would you like to marry me, young girl?'

Yvonne was astonished, and could hardly speak for shyness and embarrassment. 'I do not know what to say, but I can tell you that my life at home is miserable.' And she lowered her eyes to cry. The shining handsome stranger asked her to think about his proposal, and to meet him in the same place at sunrise the next morning. And with this request, he disappeared from her sight.

At sunset Yvonne drove her cows and sheep home, but now she was singing merrily for the first time in her life! Her family were amazed and wondered aloud what had made such a change in her. When she had put the cows in the byre and the sheep in the fold, she told her mother about the young man, and asked her for motherly advice, for she did not know what to say to him.

'You are a fool,' said her mother cruelly, 'full of nonsense and fancy tales. And even if a young man did ask you to marry him, why make an unhappy life even worse? Do you think that marriage is a happy dream?'

Yvonne replied, 'I'll never be as unhappy anywhere as I am here and now.' But her mother just shrugged and turned her back on her.

At sunrise the next morning Yvonne fairly danced her way to the great heath with her sheep and cows. At the very same time and place as before, the handsome young man appeared to her, and asked her to be his wife. This time she blushed, and said quickly, 'Yes, I'd like that very much.' So they went to ask for consent from her parents.

Yvonne's father, mother and brothers were momentarily struck dumb at the sight of such a fine shining prince of a man, so richly dressed and asking them if he could marry the poor glum little shepherdess. But it did not take them long to agree.

'Who are you?' asked her mother.

'On the wedding day, you will know then who I am,' replied the prince.

So they appointed a day and the young man left them all in a state of astonishment, rushing to prepare for the wedding.

On the wedding day, the prince returned with a best man almost as good-looking as himself, riding in a golden carriage pulled by four magnificent white horses, and the entire outfit was so highly adorned that it shone like the sun, illuminating everything they passed. The wedding ceremony was the grandest that anyone in that district had ever seen, and there was a great feast afterwards, supplied by the groom. But as soon as he rose from the table, the prince told his new bride to climb straight away into the shining carriage and go to his palace without delay.

Yvonne asked if she might gather her clothing and belongings, but her husband replied, 'You will need to take nothing with you, for everything that you could wish for will be found in my palace.'

So she climbed into the shining carriage, and as they were leaving, her brothers shouted after her, asking where they could find her when they wished to visit her.

'At the Palace of Crystal, on the far side of the Black Sea,' was the reply.

A year went by and the six brothers became anxious for news of their little sister. The five older brothers decided to mount their finest horses and seek her out, but they forced the youngest, Yvon, to stay behind at home, saying he was too stupid, and would slow them down, and would fall off any horse. The five brothers rode and rode, always towards the rising sun, which was the direction the shining carriage had taken. They asked everyone they met for directions to the Palace of Crystal, but no one could help them.

They travelled into strange countries unknown to them and came at last to the edge of a vast forest. There they met an ancient woodsman and asked him if he knew of the Palace of Crystal.

'There's a long ride in the forest, which is called the lane of the Palace of Crystal. I've never been along it, for it goes too far for my old legs and I might never come back. Perhaps that ride leads to the place you seek.'

The five brothers rode boldly into the forest and they found the wide lane between the trees. They had not gone far when they heard a terrifying sound like thunder above their heads, roaring through the tree-tops, with flashes like lightning. They were afraid and their horses tried to bolt. Finally the thunder claps and flashes of light stopped, and they went on deeper into the forest. Night fell and they began to fear wild beasts.

One of the brothers climbed a tall tree, looking for the Palace of Crystal, for surely they must be near it by now, it or any other dwelling. But all around were nothing but trees, as far as his eye could behold in the waning light. So he climbed down and they rode on through the shadows, until they could hardly see the way ahead. Another brother climbed a tree and this time he saw something.

'What can you see?' called his brothers.

'I can see a huge fire burning, over there!' He threw his hat in the direction of the fire and they travelled that way, hoping there were people and food and shelter by the fire. Once again they heard the thunderous noise overhead, louder than before. The trees creaked and swayed and crashed against one another, while shattered branches and splinters of wood fell all about them. And what thunder, what lightning, what terror! At the very peak of the terror, there came a sudden silence, and the night was serene and calm.

The brothers made their way towards the fire, following the flight of the hat, and when they reached it, they saw an ancient crone with a beard and long rattling teeth, throwing logs into the flames.

The oldest brother, minding his manners for once, said, 'Good evening, Granny, do you know the way to the Palace of Crystal?'

'Yes, in truth I do;' she replied. 'But you wait here until my eldest son returns, for he goes there every day, and brings back the latest news from that place. He's away there now, but soon he'll be back, soon enough. Perhaps you boys have seen him in the forest?'

'We have seen no one, not a soul all night.'

'Surely you heard him then, for everyone hears him when he passes thorough the woods. But wait! Here he comes now. Can't you hear him coming?'

And they heard again the thunderous roaring, growing louder and louder.

'Hide yourselves, quick! Get in under the branches, for my little son is always hungry when he returns, and I fear that he might eat first and answer questions last.'

Shaking with terror, the five brothers hid under the bushes in the dark, and as the last of them squeezed into a thorny bush, a huge giant came down from the sky, bending double to touch the ground. As soon as he had done so, he snuffled and sniffled all about him, like a pig after truffles.

'I smell the stink of Christians here, Mummy, and I must eat them, I'm so famished.' His roaring voice shook the trees and blew away stones. The brothers clung together in the cosy thorns, wishing they had stayed at home.

But the grandmother lifted up a huge club and shook it in the face of the giant, saying, 'You try to eat everything, you silly boy. Just you watch out that you don't catch the wrong end of my little stick! You'll catch it all right if you do any harm to my nephews, the sons of my dear sister, these fine well-behaved boys who have come to pay their respects to me!'

The giant trembled at her threats, and swore that he would do no harm to his dear cousins, no matter how tasty they were, no, not even with a little garlic butter. So the crone bid the five brothers show themselves, and she introduced them formally to her giant son.

'Yes, well, they are delightful, but are they not rather . . . well, *small*?' he asked. He could not eat his own cousins, after all, but he could hardly believe that they were family.

'You will not harm one greasy hair on their little curly heads,' said Granny. 'And what's more, you are going to do them a favour!'

'I am?' said the giant. 'And what kind of favour might it be? Do they need fattening up, some healthy food, some decent drink to stiffen them and make them grow?'

'They are looking for their sister, who has gone to the Palace of Crystal. You are going to lead them to her.'

'No, no, it is too far for my little legs, Mummy,' roared the giant. 'But I'm willing to lead them a good part of the way, and then point them in the right direction for the rest.'

And so it was agreed, and the brothers thanked the giant, who bid them lie down by the blazing fire to sleep, for they had to start well before dawn. The brothers lay trembling by the fire, pretending to sleep, each terrified that he would be toasted as a dainty morsel and eaten. They watched the giant through half-closed eyes, as he ate a stack of whole seared sheep, each one being but a mouthful.

Just before midnight the giant woke the brothers, saying, 'Come on, cousins, it is time to take your journey.' He spread a huge black sheet upon the ground, and told the brothers to mount their horses and have them stand upon it. Then the giant walked into heart of the fire, and his mother threw great logs and whole tree trunks upon it. As the fire grew, they heard the roaring thunderous noise that they had heard twice before in the forest. Gradually, the sheet lifted the brothers, still mounted on their horses, off the forest floor. And when the giant's clothing was all burned away, he too rose up into the air, like a huge fireball, and then the black sheet followed him speedily. They flew at a terrifying pace for a long time, until they landed upon a great plain that stretched away in all directions.

Half of this plain was burnt dry, while the other half was covered in lush, tall grass. In the arid desert was a herd of strong, shining horses, while in the fertile grass a herd of thin, worn-out nags staggered about trying to bite one another.

The flaming giant left the brothers where the plain divided, saying that he could take them no further. When their horses stepped off the black sheet and on to the plain, they died instantly. In despair the brothers tried to catch some of the fine horses from the desert, but they could not even get close to them, so fast did they run. Next they chased after the starving nags, which were easy to catch and mount but soon took them into the gorse and thorn bushes at the boundary of the lush land and the desert, and threw them off.

Cut and bleeding, in despair, they gave up their quest and decided to return home.

'We should go home,' said the eldest. 'This accursed palace is not for us.' And so they trudged back, following the light of the setting sun for many weeks, living off the land, until they came to the great forest. They avoided the campsite of the old crone and her giant son, and passed through the forest rapidly, more rapidly, it seemed to them, than when they had travelled in the other direction.

At last they returned home and told all that happened to them. Their little brother, Yvon, was sitting on a round stone, close to the fire. When he heard their tale, he said, 'Let me try this adventure! It's my turn to try now, and I swear that I will not return without seeing my dear sister!'

The brothers called him an idiot, an imbecile, a fool.

'I may be all of those, but I will find her, wherever she may be.'

So they gave him a worn-out old mare and he set off alone. He went the same way as his brothers, in the direction of the sun at dawn. In time he reached the great forest and came to the long ride called the lane of the Palace of Crystal. At its entrance he met an old woman, who demanded to know where he thought he was going.

'To see my sister, dear granny, who lives in the Palace of Crystal?' The crone smiled at him and clicked her long teeth together in a kindly manner.

'Well, if she is your sister, then I can tell you straight; don't take this route, but take that one over there!' And she pointed to a hidden path that he had not seen, quite different from the wide open lane. 'You follow that path until you reach a great plain, and you go along the edge of the plain until you find a black road of earth. You take that black earthy road, and no matter what you see or hear, even if it burns with flames, go straight ahead. Go straight ahead without fear and you shall reach the Palace of Crystal and see your sister again.'

Young Yvon thanked the grandmother, and he took the path that she had shown him. He reached the plain quickly, as it seemed, and found the black earth road. The entrance was filled with a mass of writhing snakes, so he was afraid and hesitated. His horse was fearful too, but he remembered what the old woman had told him and spurred his horse on. Straight away the serpents coiled around the legs of his mount and bit it until it died. Yvon fell into the mass of serpents, but they did not bite him. He picked himself up and strode to the end of the road unharmed, for his fear had left him.

Now he found himself on the shore of a great lake, with no ferry, and he was unable to swim. So he walked bravely into the water, for he had sworn not to return until he had seen his sister. It came up to his knees, then to his armpits, then to his chin and soon it lapped over his head. But he kept on walking, and crossed that great water unharmed, for his intent kept him from drowning.

On the other side of the lake he came to a narrow dark path, full of stout thorns and brambles, deeply rooted on both sides. He thought that he might never get through, but he was determined not to give up. Yvon crawled on all fours like a snake to get through this narrow thorny way, until his clothing was all torn away, and his skin cut and bleeding. And despite all the difficulties, his determination saw him through. Further on, when he emerged from the deep thorns, he saw a thin spindly horse galloping to meet him. This horse stopped, inviting him to mount, and to his great surprise he saw that it was his own, the very horse that he had thought dead. He was filled with joy and climbed upon its back, saying, 'A thousand blessings upon you, dear little horse, for I cannot walk on alone.'

Next they came to a place where there was a large stone laid upon two upright stones, a dolmen. The horse stopped and struck its hoof upon the large stone, which tilted to reveal a tunnel. A voice from deep within said, 'Dismount and enter.'

Yvon obeyed the voice and went into the dark tunnel. It stank of poisonous reptiles and was so dark that he had to feel his way forward, for he could see nothing. Behind him in the dark, he heard a noise which grew louder and louder, as if a horde of demons came after him. But at the same time he saw a glimmer of light ahead, which gave him hope. The noises drew close, but so did the light. And suddenly he burst out of that tunnel, safe and sound.

Now he was at a crossroads and did not know which road to take. So he went straight on, following the road opposite the tunnel exit. Over this road were set many high gates and they were all locked. He was unable to open them, so he climbed over the top of each one, up the posts and over. At last the road went downhill, and Yvon saw that everything

Dolmen: such stone structures are associated traditionally with druids, and with Otherworld or poetic inspiration

at the end of the road was made of crystal. He saw a crystal palace, a crystal sky and a crystal sun.

'They say that my sister, Yvonne, lives in the crystal palace, so I am near to the end of my long journey. It is all true.'

When he reached the Palace of Crystal, it was radiant with light and his eyes watered. He went into the courtyard, where everything shone brilliantly. There were many doors and they were all locked. But he slid down a little vent into the cellar and from underground he went up into the great hall of that place, filled with light. This hall had six doors leading into it, one after the other, and each one opened at Yvon's touch. Beyond the first hall, he came to a second of greater beauty, which had three doors. Each of these doors opened into another beautiful hall. In the last hall, the most beautiful of all, he saw his sister sleeping on a golden bed. He gazed admiringly at her, unable to move for a long time. Evening came and still she did not awaken.

Yvon heard footsteps, and the sound of little bells ringing with every step, and into the hall came a handsome young man. He went straight to the sleeping beauty and gave her three hard, loud slaps. Then he lay beside her upon the bed. Yvon was embarrassed, uncertain what to do, but he stayed for the sake of his sister. Eventually the young husband fell asleep by the side of his wife. It was then that Yvon realized there was no sound in the miraculous palace and no hunger. He had arrived with a prodigious appetite and now he had none. Night passed in total silence, and at dawn the husband awoke, and gave his wife three hard slaps. Once again, she did not awaken or even twitch at the blows. Then her husband departed.

Yvon sat bemused in his corner, fearing that his sister was dead. So he leaned over her and gave her a last kiss, whereupon she suddenly awakened and said, 'What joy to see you again, dear brother.' And they embraced one another tenderly.

Yvon asked where her husband was.

'He is away on his travels.'

'Has he been gone long?'

'No, he left a few moments ago.'

'Poor sister, you must be so unhappy with him.'

'But I am very happy with him, brother.'

'You cannot be so, I saw him give you three hard slaps last night and another three this morning.'

'Slaps? What are you saying? Those were kisses. He kisses me every night and morning.'

'Strange kisses, I think they are. And why is there no hunger here?'

Since arriving I have not felt cold or hot, hungry or thirsty, nor have I needed anything nor experienced any discomfort.'

'And is it only yourself and your husband in this palace?'

'Oh, no, there are many others here whom I saw clearly when I arrived, but because I spoke to them when I had been told not to, they disappeared.'

So Yvon and Yvonne spent the day together, in the silent brightness of that palace. They talked about their family, their homeland and other familiar things, so far away. When Yvonne's husband arrived that evening he was pleased to see his brother-in-law. Yvon told him of the trials that he had undergone to reach the Palace of Crystal, and was pleased when he said, 'Not many can come this far, but you can go back more easily, and I will help you through the worst parts of the journey.'

Every day that Yvon stayed, his sister's husband left early in the morning, without saying where he went, and returned after sunset. Yvon was intrigued by this mystery and he asked his sister if she knew where her husband went each day.

'I do not know,' she replied, 'I have never asked and he has never told me.'

Next morning, Yvon confronted his brother-in-law and said, 'I'd like to go with you on your travels today, to get some air, to see your wonderful country. May I come with you?'

'You may, but on the condition that you do as I say.'

'I promise to obey your instructions.'

'Listen carefully, for you must not touch anything as we travel and you must speak only to me, no matter what you hear or see.'

Yvon agreed, and they left the palace by a path so narrow that he had to walk behind his sister's husband. First they came to a dry, sandy plain with fat, healthy cattle sitting on the sand, gently chewing their cud.

Next they came to a plain with lush, tall grass, with many thin cattle bellowing and fighting one another.

Yvon asked, 'What does this mean, fat cattle on sand, thin cattle on grass?'

'The fat cattle are the poor who do not covet the goods of others, but the thin cattle are the rich who can never be satisfied.'

Further on they saw two trees contesting so bitterly that splinters of wood flew when they clashed together. Yvon was carrying a staff and he held it up between them. 'Stop bringing pain to one another, stop fighting and live in peace,' he cried.

They immediately changed into man and woman, and showered blessings upon him. 'We have been fighting for three centuries, for no one had pity on us. When we were married in the mortal world we fought all the time, and our punishment has been to fight as trees for ever unless a kind soul should say a good word to us. Our suffering is over at last, and we will go to paradise, and we will see you there one day.' With this statement, they instantly disappeared.

Next Yvon heard a frightening noise, yells, shouts, curses, grinding of teeth, rattling of chains, until he thought the very blood in his veins would curdle with fear.

'What is all this?' he asked his brother-in-law.

'We have come at last to the entrance to Hell, but we can go no further together as a result of your disobedience. You spoke directly to the two trees, even though I instructed you to deal with no one but me, neither talking nor touching. I will go further on alone, but you must go back to your sister. When I return I'll direct you homeward at last.'

So Yvon retraced his steps to the Palace of Crystal, very sorry for himself for being so foolish and having to turn back. But his brother-in-law went on into the Underworld alone.

'What this?' cried Yvonne when she saw her brother. 'Back so soon?'

'Yes, indeed, dear sister' he muttered sadly. She questioned him strictly, and he told her how he had disobeyed her husband and talked to the two trees.

'And still you do not know where he goes?'

'No, I do not, only that it is in the Underworld, beyond the gates of suffering and revenge.'

When the brother-in-law returned at his usual time, he ordered Yvon to leave.

'You broke your vow of silence. and now you must return to your own country for a while. When you return here again, it shall be for ever, so go down that road without fear, knowing that you will be back soon.'

Yvon followed the road that he had been shown and nothing hindered him on the journey back. He was not hungry, he was not thirsty, he was not tired and so did not sleep. He walked without stopping, knowing no fatigue, and at last he came into his own realm. But where he expected to find his father's house, there was a large field, and old huge beeches and oaks all around it.

So he went to a nearby house that he had seen and asked for his father by name, and his name was Ewen Dagorn.

'Dagorn . . . Ewen Dagorn?' they all muttered. 'No, there is no one by that name around here, boy.' Then an old man, nodding and dribbling in the fireplace where it was warm, croaked out, 'Ewen Dagorn, yes. When I was a lad I heard my grandfather speak of him as someone who had been dead a long time, and his children, and his children's children. There are no more Dagorns left, young man.'

Yvon was astounded. Realizing that he knew no one, and no one knew him, he went to the graveyard to seek out his family. Some of the graves with the name of Dagorn were over 300 years old. So he went into the ancient little church and prayed to die, which prayer was granted, and he surely joined his sister in the Palace of Crystal.

From Breton oral tradition, collected and published by F. M. Luzel in
Contes Populaires de Basse-Bretagne, Paris, 1879
(English version by R. J. Stewart)

*Here ends the First Part, that of The Cauldron – Wisdom Through
Questing – The Dark Goddess*

PART TWO

The Sacred Head

◆

Wisdom Through Suffering

◆

The Sacred King and Poet

INTRODUCTION

R. J. Stewart

he old Celtic and pre-Celtic religions, myths and ritual practices merged together through the centuries, generating a holism of tradition handed down to the present day in folklore. The druids took many of the magical and religious traditions found among the Celtic races and refined them into a specific set of practices, probably coming into focus as an aristocratic body with specific membership, training and authority before the first Roman incursions into Celtic territory. The remains of druidic rituals, metaphysics and cosmology, prophecy and the arts of ceremonial judgement and of advising kings, were later found in a variety of interconnected forms within bardic tradition.

Such bardic traditions existed in Wales as late as the nineteenth and early twentieth centuries, preserved not only in manuscripts in private ownership but also in oral tradition in both rural and industrial communities. The story, song and music aspects of the tradition were also kept alive in Brittany, where distinctly 'primal' material, particularly lore concerning death and the Underworld, survived centuries of oppression.

In Scotland we find Lowland ballads and tales in Scottish English that relate closely to ancient magical themes and to more historically defined Welsh bardic tradition. This is not surprising, for one of the great flowering periods of bardic poetry was between the sixth and eighth centuries, when Lowland Scotland and most of Wales were one kingdom, speaking a mainly Welsh language rather than Scottish Gaelic. Much of the Taliesin and Merlin material was refined at this time, hence the traditions of Merlin and Arthur in Lowland Scotland as well as in north Wales.

In the Scottish Highlands and Islands, we find a different though related tradition, essentially the same as that of Ireland. Long interlaced stories are a feature of Scottish oral lore, and these were still found as late as the 1950s. Such tales are linked closely to the themes found in medieval Irish texts, which are the sources for much of our knowledge of early Celtic tradition, yet the Scottish Gaelic storytellers had no knowledge of such texts, either in their original form or in English translation. The heroic, epic, magical tales were kept alive solely through family tradition, surviving beyond the demise of the travelling bards or poets of earlier centuries.

In Ireland, as in Scotland, oral tradition includes tales and songs from the venerable poetic traditions, once the lore of druids, then the art of the itinerant poets and teachers, and finally the property of ordinary country people. Once again we might emphasize a family theme, for songs and tales are preserved in certain families,

The king in the tree

as are obscure ceremonies and customs, such as those relating to holy wells and sacred skulls. This family aspect of the tradition may be the oldest of all, a tribal preservation of wisdom, and it ultimately survived and replaced the specialist practices of the trained druid, bard or poet.

Thus the information handed down to us is filtered through many centuries of use and through the varied viewpoints of those embodying and, at second-hand, reporting the druidic and bardic traditions. Sadly, much of our earliest source information is from hostile or romantic commentators, such as classical historians or early Christian writers. These may be compared, however, with the many examples of Celtic tradition that were written down from the early medieval period onwards, and from folklore right into the twentieth century.

The Sacred Head

Out of the complex interlaced source material, there are a small number of themes that are at the very foundation of Celtic mythology, and were undoubtedly incorporated into druidic practices, though they probably come from pre-druidic religion, having their counterparts worldwide. These themes may be summarized as follows:

1 The quest through, and knowledge of, the three worlds: Overworld, Middle World and Underworld (see page 25). The Overworld is that of the moon, sun, planets and stars, the celestial and sky deities. The Middle World is that of our planetary surface, with humans, animals, birds, fish, plants and natural forms – seas, mountains, rivers, rocks, springs and so forth. The Middle World is also inhabited by spiritual beings, inherent within many forms, sometimes partaking of the other two worlds.

The Underworld is within the body of the land, and deeper into the planet. Here are found the faery races, deities of the land and planet, creatures such as giants (Titans in Greek myth), ancestral powers and other mythic or spirit beings. Indeed, the Underworld is the most potent spiritual realm of Celtic tradition, home of the Dark Mother of death and regeneration.

Questing through and gaining knowledge of the three worlds comprise the greater part of Celtic tradition, and are central to what we know of druidic and bardic spiritual lore. In folk tradition we find that descriptions of the three realms vary considerably, particularly where there has been a Christian influence at work in the culture.

2 Sub-themes found linked to the awareness and interaction of the three worlds are the Sacred Kingship and the Sacred Head. Sometimes these two are interlinked, as they often involve a deep bond with the land, manifesting as a union between the male king of sacrifice and the goddess of birth, death and regeneration.

The druids' role seems to have been to advise kings and to help in their magical selection through traditional ceremonies. In ancient Ireland kings were strictly limited by complex taboos and were constantly advised on the protocols of kingship by druids. This is reflected in a rather distorted way by the medieval idea of the sage Merlin first training and later advising King Arthur. The earliest sources, however, tell of a boy Merlin who utters prophecies, and later of a mad prince Merlin who lives with the wild animals in the forest – themes more connected to the direct experience of the three worlds than to sacred kingship.

By the time we find such traditions in bardic poems and tales, and in the literature of the Middle Ages, they are reported as wondrous events and adventures rather than as literal religious practices or philosophical teachings.

One of the bardic themes of particular significance, which reaches back to primal Celtic religion and magic, was that of the sacred prophetic head. It filters into the medieval Grail legends in the story of Peredur, who sees a procession bearing a severed head, a platter and a bleeding lance. These are variants of the four wonders or weapons of the Tuatha Dé Danann in Irish legend, the sacred blade, spear, cauldron and stone. The cauldron, from which the Grail as a vessel is taken, is of major significance in Celtic myth as the eternal vessel of regeneration.

The severed head is found in the legend of Cuchulain, where only he is brave enough to accept the challenge of cutting off a giant's head, and the story is reworked in the English legend of Gawain and the Green Knight. When the giant's head is severed, he picks it up and walks away, and the hero must keep an appointment next year to receive his own blow from the giant.

The classic example of the sacred head, kingship and prophecy is found in *The Mabinogion*, in the tale of Bran and Branwen, the children of Llyr. During a terrible war with the Irish, Bran is fatally wounded in the foot or thigh. His last instructions to his comrades are to cut off his head and carry it with them, after burying his body. He foretells that after much travelling they will settle on an island (off the coast of Pembrokeshire) where the head will speak to them. The company, known as the Assembly of the Wondrous Head, then dwell in a hall with doors open to certain directions but closed to others. While they are there, they have no memory of sorrow or suffering, and are entertained by feasting, by the utterances of the head of Bran and by the magical birds of Rhiannon singing sweetly.

As Bran prophesied, one of the company opens a forbidden door leading to the west, and they remember all their suffering. They also remember the prophecy, and set out, as predicted/ instructed, to bury the head in the east of the country, upon the White Hill (traditionally associated with the site of the Tower of London).

There are several other sites associated with Bran outside of Wales, such as the steep Brandon Hill located in Bristol (a look-out place that commands a good view of the River Avon) and Brent Knoll in Somerset (also a look-out place, and a large prehistoric hill-top site, commanding the entrance to the Glastonbury marshes from the Severn estuary).

The ancient association of Bran with guardianship and protection is stated in the *Mabinogion*, for as long as his head is buried on the White Hill, no invaders will come from across the sea. The burial of the head is described as one of three fortunate concealments in the 'Triads' and elsewhere, while its disinternment by Arthur is described as one of the three unfortunate disclosures, bringing sorrow upon the land.

Bran is a primal guardian diety, described as being of giant size, able to wade the Irish Sea. He is also associated with music, for he carries the bards and minstrels on his back, and with the act of bridging, for he uses his body as a bridge for the army to cross over the River Liffey. The connection with music, poetry and bridging are given as puns in the *Mabinogion*, yet they contain traditional teachings regarding sacred kingship. The Roman high priest was called *pontifex maximus*, a title still used today by the pope, the great bridge-maker. Curiously, the Capitol in Rome, a high hill with the most ancient shrines upon it, was the site of a sacred buried head in Roman tradition.

We have used the famous example of Bran as it encapsulates the ideas of prophecy, kingship, guardianship and an otherworldly state of bliss and forgetfulness. The head bridges between this Otherworld and the human world, reminding the company that they must be responsible in their own realm.

The sacred head appears in a number of Irish legends, in addition to the Cuchulain story mentioned, for the early Irish warriors were head-hunters and preserved the dried heads of their opponents. The Celts of Gaul, according to classical historians, kept heads preserved in cedarwood boxes. The remains of an early Celtic shrine in France show a trilithon gate with niches for skulls.

The idea of the sacred head is found in folklore and customs in Britain and Ireland into the twentieth century, often in association with wells or shrines. Certain hallowed sites kept skulls which were used for healing rituals, as vessels or cups. In the popular folk tale 'The King of Colchester's Daughter' we have an English version of a widespread story about a girl who raises three heads from a deep well. One is bronze, one silver and one gold, and she combs their hair and sings to them. These heads are embodiments of three levels of the Underworld, a classic triplicity.

A satisfying connection between modern archaeology, ancient legend, sacred kingship and Celtic religion is found at Aquae Sulis, the Roman name for Bath, England. In his legendary *Historia Regum Britanniae* Geoffrey of Monmouth reports that King Bladud, grandfather of Bran and Branwen, founded the site and taught the druidic arts of ancestor magic and flight, eventually crashing to his death on the site of what is now London (the name *Bladud* means 'light-dark' or 'bright-shadow'). In his *Vita Merlini*, Geoffrey of Monmouth has

Opposite: Assembly of the wondrous head of Bran

Bladud and his consort Aleron ('wings') presiding over the hot springs of Bath, which are at the centre of the bardic universe described by Taliesin to Merlin, forming the gateway to the Otherworld.

On show in the museum at Bath is a superb Celtic solar head (often inaccurately called a Gorgon's head). The carving is a circular relief of an imposing male face with wild hair, long moustaches and staring eyes. He has wings on either side of his head and is surrounded by flames. Beneath his chin are two serpents, linked in the manner of a torque, the Celtic symbol of royalty. This solar deity is probably the being called Bladud in the legendary histories, connected to magic, flight and a fall from the heights to the depths. He has upon his brow the mark of the three rays, which are very often described in bardic tradition as the primal three powers of universal creation.

The goddess at Bath, presiding over the sacred hot springs, was called Sul or Sulis, which means 'eye' or 'gap' (with a sexual connotation), for she is a variant of Ceridwen, the goddess of the Underworld. The entire Celtic/Roman complex of Aquae Sulis is an excellent example of ancestral Underworld magic refined by Roman politics into a temple of Minerva.

The Meaning of the Sacred Head

It is likely that there is no one 'true' meaning of the sacred head, but a complex of interlinked sacro-magical, metaphysical and philosophical traditions, associated with the idea of the three worlds in Celtic tradition. We find a similar idea, interestingly, in Jewish mysticism, where the Tree of Life relates metaphysics to the human body, the solar system and the stars. The head or crown in the Cabbala is the first and last sphere of universal being, and is found in the human as well as the universal world. Ancient prophets adopted a position with the head between the knees or feet, forehead touching the earth, cloak or robe pulled over the entire body.

The sacred or prophetic head is an embodiment of the relationship between the three worlds, for it is aware in all worlds, through all time. While we may have ideas that an anthropologist would suggest originated in primitive head-hunting magic, the theme of the sacred head becomes an allegory of divine and human perception and declaration.

There is a further element to the sacred-head theme, for it is also interlinked with beliefs and practices concerning the regeneration of life, particularly with the cauldron. Titanic figures such as Bran, acting as sacred kings and guardians of the land, also partake of the mystery of the sun at midnight, light regenerating out of darkness. And this, after all, is the secret of inspiration, a sudden light born out of fruitful darkness.

THE DIALOGUE OF THE TWO SAGES

ABOUT THE TIME of Christ, when the king of Ulster was Conchobhar mac Nessa, Adna the Ollamh of Ulster died. His place was bestowed on the poet Fercheirtne, whose experience and mastery made him a more than likely candidate. But Adna's son Néde, being away to study in Scotland and unaware of Fercheirtne's appointment, learned of his father's death from the sound of the sea waves as he strolled the shore. He returned at once to Emhain Macha, capital town of Ulster, to take his father's place. The first man he met on entering the halls of Conchobhar was Bricriu, a man who loved to stir up conflict whenever he could. Bricriu undertook to bestow the ollamh position on Néde, accepting in return a valuable gift, remarking only that Néde as a beardless youth was hardly suitable. Néde plucked a tuft of grass and, uttering a verse of power, placed it against his chin, where it at once took on the appearance of a luxuriant beard. And Néde seated himself in the ollamh seat and about him he wrapped the robe of three colours: the middle part of it many bright feathers of birds, the lower part of it white bronze in colour, the upper part of it bright gold.

Now chuckling to himself, Bricriu set out to tell Fercheirtne how Néde had stolen his ollamhship, and Fercheirtne, in a fury, set out for Conchobhar's palace to deal with the interloper. But when he beheld the youth who sat in his chair, Fercheirtne was taken aback by his poise, and addressed Néde with some civility stating, however, that he was occupying he chair awarded to Fercheirtne. Néde replied with equal politeness and formality pointing out Bricriu's malicious jest, but nevertheless requesting that Fercheirtne should satisfy himself that the boy who had unwittingly usurped an already given position was, in fact, most worthy to be Ollamh of Ulster. In establishing this, Fercheirtne addressed Néde thus, as the bards relate:

> a question, o child of education
> where do you come from?

to which Néde replied:
> not hard to answer
> from a wise man's heel
> from a confluence of wisdoms
> from perfection of goodness
> from brightness of sunrise
> from poetry's hazels
> from splendour's circuits
> from that state where truth's worth is measured
> from that measure where truth is realized
> from that reality where lies are vanquished
> from where all colours are seen
> from where all art is reborn
>
> and you, my elder, where do you come from?

to which Fercheirtne replied:
> not hard to answer
> from the width of the pillars of the age
> from the fill of the rivers of Leinster

from the length of the hall of the wife of Nechtan
from the reach of the arm of the wife of Núadu
from the extent of the country of the sun
from the height of the mansions of the moon
from the stretch of a babe's umbilical cord

a question, o youth of instruction
what is your name?

to which Néde replied:
not hard to answer ·
minuscule and muckle I am
dazzling and highly hard
entitle me Fire's flame
name me Fire of Word
or Noise of Knowingness
or Fountain of Riches
or Sword of Canticles
or Ardent Verity of Genius

and you, my elder, what is your name?

to which Fercheirtne replied:
not hard to answer
of seers most sure
I am chief revealer
of that which is uttered
and that which is asked
Inquiry of the Curious
Weft of Deftness
Creel of Verse am I
and Abundance of the Sea

a question, o young man of learning
what art do you practise?

to which Néde replied:
not hard to answer
I bring blush to face
and spirit to flesh
I practise fear's erasure
and tumescence of impudence
metre's nurture
honour's venture
and wisdom's wooing
I shape beauty to human mouths
give wings to insight
I make naked the word
in small space I have foregathered
the cattle of cognizance
the stream of science
the totality of teaching
the captivation of kings
and the legacy of legend

The two sages

And you my elder, what art do you practise?

to which Fercheirtne replied:
  not hard to answer
  sifting of streams for gold of wisdom
  lulling of hearts from the fires of anger
  captaincy of words
  excellency of skill
  putting feathers in kings' pillows
  I have acquired a thirst that would drain the Boyne
  I am a maker of shields and wounds
  a slicer of pure air
  an architect of thought
  I can say much with few words
  I can sing the long miles of great heroes' lives
  I am a jeweller of the heart

  a question, O young exalted man
  what are your tasks?

to which Néde replied:
  not hard to answer
  to cross life to the mountain of youth
  to rise to the hunting of age
  to follow kings to the tomb
  to pass between the wick and the flame
  between the sword and the terror
  and you, my elder, what are your tasks?

to which Fercheirtne replied:
  not hard to answer
  to scale from honour to honour
  to attain the conversation of the wise
  to suckle at the breast of poetry
  to wade the wide rivers of the world
  to make music for the ferocious demon
  upon the slope of death

  A question, o wise man of young face
  by what path have you come?

to which Néde replied:
  not hard to answer
  by way of a king's beard
  by way of the forest
  on the back of the ploughman's ox
  upon a nourishment of acorns
  upon the barley and milk of the mother of song
  on one grain of wheat
  by way of the most narrow river crossing
  upon my own two legs

  and you, my elder
  by what path have you come?

to which Fercheirtne replied:
    not hard to answer
    by way of the whip of the many-skilled Lugh
    by way of the sweet breasts of women
    by way of the letters cut on the staff
    by way of the spear head
    and the silver dress
    upon a chariot without a wheel
    upon a wheel without a chariot
    upon the three things unknown to Mac Ind Oc
    The son of the young

    and you, young man of manly understanding
    whose son are you?

to which Néde replied:
    not hard to answer
    I am the son of Poetry
    Poetry son of Looking
    Looking son of Thought
    Thought son of Learning
    Learning son of Curiosity
    Curiosity son of Seeking
    Seeking son of Great Wisdom
    Great Wisdom son of Great Common Sense
    Great Common Sense son of True Understanding
    True Understanding son of Insight
    Insight son of the Three Gods of Poetry

    and you, my elder
    whose son are you?

to which Fercheirtne replied:
    not hard to answer
    son of the fatherless man
    buried in the womb of his mother
    blessed after his death
    married to his own death
    my father is the first cry of the babe
    the last cry of the dying
    Ailm is his name

    A question, Néde
    What news do you bring?

to which Néde replied:
    not hard to answer
    I bring good news
    seas of fish
    fullness of lakes
    glad countenance of glades
    wood at work
    fruit boughs bending
    barley bearded

bees swarming
joyful land
peaceful peace
merry weather
soldiers paid wages
kings sitting in sunlight
war distant
art present
men boasting
women sewing
thorn trees spiky
caskets of gold
a bravery for every boast
enough thread for every stitch
every good thing I sing
for ever
there is none greater
than the Great Creator
the same who revealed
at first
the nine hazels of poetry
who made also
the rank of Ollamh
for in the world I have
three real fathers
my father in flesh
Adne who is dead
my father in Art
Eochu Horsemouth
who is in Scotland
and my father in years
Fercheirtne.

Then Néde rose from the ollamh seat, handing as he did so the poet's
many-coloured robe to Fercheirtne, and Fercheirtne said:
great poet, wise young man
son of Adne
may you get glory from men and gods
may you be the greatest treasure,
of Emain Macha, Ollamh of Ulster.

And Néde replied:
may that same glory be yours
Ollamh of Ulster.

From Irish tradition
(English version by Robin Williamson)

DAN DHEIRG
(SONG OF THE RED)

Gach dan gu dan an Dheirg
Gach eachdraigh gu eachdraigh Chonnail
Gach laoidh gu laoidh amadan mhoir
S'gach moladh gu moladh loch Ce

Every song must be compared to the song of the red,
Every history to the history of Connal
Every lay to the lay of the Great Fool
And every praise to the praise of Loch Ce

Highland saying

BECAUSE THERE ARE more ways than one to tell the story and more than one to skin a cat, I will tell you the tale of the Dan Dheirg as they used to tell it in Glen Shee, where my father's people lived long ago, before they went to Ulster. Like many another story, the Dan Dheirg has to do with Fionn. For it is said and said truly of the hero Fionn MacCumbhail that if one day goes by without his name being mentioned, the world will come to an end.

Fionn was the leader of the Fianna, the warriors of Erin who hunted the great forests of Scotland and Ireland. *Naoi mile gaisgeach glan,* 9,000 perfect heroes. His dog Bran was the greatest dog in the world, his son Ossian was the greatest bard in the world, his sword, the Son of the Moon, was the greatest sword in the world. Fionn could acquire all magic power by chewing on his thumb. But he didn't always remember to do it.

It is said of Fionn's generosity that his house was the stranger's home and if the leaves of the forests of the world were red gold and the waters of the world were white silver, Fionn would have given them all away. But being a man, Fionn had his weakness. That weakness was jealousy.

Fionn had three wives, in his life. The first, Saba, was put under spells into the shape of a deer by a druid called the Dark. It was as a deer that she bore Fionn's son Ossian, whose name means Son of the Deer. Saba never returned to the human world.

In the last years of his life, Fionn married his third wife, Oonagh. Oonagh outlived him.

But it is of his second wife this story tells. Her name was Grainne. She was a beautiful woman, of course, and the daughter of King Cormac. Her father and herself were very pleased with the match. She was a lot younger than Fionn. Maybe she was a lot cleverer.

What is more plentiful than the grass?
This question Fionn asked of Grainne
The dew. On every blade are many drops
This answer she gave back to him

What is hotter than fire, quicker than wind?
This question Fionn asked of Grainne
The thought of a woman between two men
This answer she gave back to him

Blacker than the crow, whiter than the snow?
This question Fionn asked of Grainne
Death, is blacker. Truth is whiter
This answer she gave back to him

What ship is fit for every cargo?
This question Fionn asked of Grainne
A blacksmith's tongs that carry hot or cold
This answer she gave back to him

What binds faster than any fetter?
This question Fionn asked of Grainne
The face and the body of her lover
Bind a woman's loving eye
More fast than destiny
This answer she gave back to him

What blush is redder than blood?
This question Fionn asked of Grainne
The face of a man shamed before his guests
This answer she gave back to him

What is more pointed than a spear?
This question Fionn asked of Grainne
The hatred of an enemy
This answer she gave back to him

What is the best of food?
This question Fionn asked of Grainne
Milk which is both food and drink
Nourishment for babes and old men
This answer she gave back to him

What is the most valuable treasure?
This question Fionn asked of Grainne
A good sword well wielded
This answer she gave back to him

What is lighter than sow-thistledown?
This question Fionn asked of Grainne
The word of a fool
This answer she gave back to him

What is softer than the down of a woman's cheek?
This question Fionn asked of Grainne
The palm that strokes it
This answer she gave back to him

What is the best way for a hero?
This question Fionn asked of Grainne
High deeds and low conceits
This answer she gave back to him.

As they were talking, Fionn's greatest friends were by them and they were drinking mead. Diarmuid was among them. One of Fionn's nephews and one of the greatest heroes of Erin, he was under two obligations of the kind that are called *gaessa*:

That he would never refuse the request of Fionn.

That he would never hunt wild boar.

The druids foretold that in his life he would be under three *gaessa*.

He had the name Diarmuid of the Love Spot, for he had a small mark on his forehead and he had to keep that covered with his hat for if any woman saw it, she would fall passionately in love with him. It so chanced that in the passing of the mead horn the hat slipped back on his head. Grainne saw the *ball searc*, the love spot. Grainne fell in love with Diarmuid.

Late that night, she came to him and she placed him under the *gaessa* that was his third obligation, that he would elope with her that very night, away rom the Hall of Fionn. They took ship and crossed the ocean into Kintyre and journeyed until they came at last to Glen Shee. There they slept under a rowan tree, not as man and wife but as brother and sister, for Diarmuid honoured Fionn.

Fionn chewed his thumb, skin to the flesh, flesh to the bone, bone to the marrow, and he could see where they were lying. He called his chief druid to him and by art sent a wakeless slumber upon Diarmuid. And he sent also a covering of blood about him so that he seemed wounded and dead. When Grainne awoke and saw her beloved so, her heart failed in her breast and the life that was in her went away from her and she died.

The Dan Dheirg was the air made upon her lamentation for Diarmuid by the bard Ullin, who was bard of the Flan before Ossian. But Diarmuid was not dead, nor was he covered in blood when he awoke and found the corpse of Grainne by him.

Messengers came to him with a request from Fionn: 'Hunt out and kill the great boar of Ben Gulbin.'

Diarmuid climbed the scree above the hill and the cliff above the scree till he roused the great boar from its lair. Bristles upon its broad back were more pointed than the spear, for the boar's bristles had the sharpness of the hatred of Fionn.

Diarmuid's spear broke on the side of the boar. It was with his sword he killed it. Fionn came up to him. 'Pace out the length of the boar for me.' In pacing the length of the boar's back, a bristle pierced Diarmuid's heel and his death rose about him like a mist.

Diarmuid said to Fionn, 'If you fetch me water in your cupped hands, my life will be restored to me.'

Fionn's anger left him as he looked into Diarmuid's blue-grey eyes. He thought of the many times the sword of Diarmuid had shielded him. He thought of the many adventures they had shared. He went to fetch the water. But as he returned from the spring, he thought of Grainne. He let the water trickle through his fingers. Diarmuid died.

From Scottish/Irish Gaelic tradition
(English version by Robin Williamson)

Several hills in Scotland have a cleft called the Boar's Scratch, named after this sad legend. The clan Campbell in Argyll have a boar's crest in their coat of arms and claim descent from Diarmuid. The tune of the Dan Dheirg was noted down by Patrick MacDonald, minister of Kilmore in Argyllshire in 1784. It forms part of a vast oral tradition of Ossianic stories in Scotland, but is one of the rare instances where the melody appropriate to the recitation has been recorded.

Music for the traditional air 'Dan Dheirg'

◆

LAMENT OF THE OLD MAN

ALL ANCIENT TALES – sagas, hero exploits, romances, wooings, cattle raids, elopements, voyages – were originally embellished with speech poems or songs to outline monologue or dialogue or to enhance descriptions. This was the custom throughout the Middle Ages. Musical accompaniment to story-telling is hinted at throughout the Celtic material, but the early style and tight language of the old Irish verses and the old Welsh *englyn* three-lined form were obscure to later generations of listeners and are left out increasingly or rewritten by about the fifteenth or sixteenth century.

Welsh poems attributed to Llywarch Hen probably date from the ninth century AD although Llywarch himself is thought to have lived about the sixth century AD. The remaining poems are all that is left, according to Ifor Williams, of a vast prose saga concerning the death of Llywarch's 24 sons in Welsh border warfare in the regions of what are now Chester, Shrewsbury and Hereford. The 'Lament of the Old Man' is the ending poem spoken by Llywarch Hen as a character in his own saga. The author is unknown.

Before my back bent
I was a spear of battle
Now I stoop with tears

Little stick, it is autumn at last
Bracken brown grass sere

What I love is passed.

Little stick, it is winter at last
Men boast and swill red beer
No one comes near my bed

Little stick, it is spring at last
Cuckoos sing in the evening light
No girl loves the sight of me

Little stick, it is May at last
Furrows red, green wheat
I sigh to see my crooked stick's beak

Little stick, kind staff
Bear up a daft old man
Llywarch Hen maundering, mumbling

A leaf blows in the wind
A life blows like a leaf away
Old now, born a year

What I loved when young
I hate now
A woman, a guest, a young horse

All that I hated then
Now visits me
Age, sickness, remorse

Nor sleep, nor joy for me
Since my sons are dead before me
I am old
Wyf hen
Wyf hen
I am old.

From Welsh tradition
(English version by Robin Williamson)

◆
PRINCESS MARCASSA

Introduction by R. J. Stewart

As in our other Breton tale, 'The Palace of Crystal', the themes of a quest and a journey through different realms or dimensions are featured. The idea of a great treasure or treasure within a threefold castle is of ancient religious significance to the Celts, and there are many echoes in this folk tale from oral tradition, reminiscent of the Grail legends of medieval literature.

Such folktales are independent of Grail texts, and were handed down among mainly illiterate people. Indeed, they often preserve an older, more pagan, set of beliefs concerning the Otherworld, with little or only token Christianizing. The Grail texts are reworkings of pagan Celtic themes of spiritual regeneration that were extensively developed by bards and story-tellers, and later preserved orally through the centuries. The Grail texts are attempts to bring Christian mysticism into a large and widespread legendary tradition.

The quest for the mysterious Dredaine bird is undertaken to heal a sick and ageing king. The castle where this wonder resides is guarded by three walls and three courtyards, filled with monstrous creatures. There is also a sleeping princess, which links the tale to the other major Celtic theme of sleepers, perhaps best known in the Germanic variant of 'Sleeping Beauty'. It is interesting to find that the ageing king thinks he can be restored by making love to the sleeping princess, something that has already been done by the hero (his youngest son), who therefore becomes king after many tribulations and tests. Here we have the idea of the Sacred Kingship and the Sovereign Goddess, which is well developed in Irish tradition. The king must wed the land, or an embodiment of the goddess of the land.

The elements of bread and wine, miraculously renewed, are found in many faery tales and predate the Christian Mass, which simply took up an established ancient ceremony of transubstantiation and the sacred feast, long established in the Mysteries and in pagan religion. There is also a magical sword to be won by our hero, reminiscent of the idea of Excalibur in Arthurian tales.

The triple courtyards, the triple rooms filled with wonders and the miraculous items obtained, are typical of the bardic quest. But our hero gives them all away, leaving them as a trail for the princess to come to him, out of the Otherworld and into the human world. There is an amusing touch in the traditional tale, for the interim land, between Britanny and the castle of wonders, is that of the Saxons, or England. In this land, the older brothers become idle drunks. Yet we can take this notion into an older strata altogether, for Britain was described in classical times as the home of druidism, where the greatest druidic mysteries were learned and from where druidic teachings were passed into mainland Europe.

THE KING OF FRANCE had three sons; the older two were handsome, strong and energetic, but the youngest was weak and sickly. He always stayed in the chimney corner by the warmth of the fire, so he was called Luduenn, which means Little Cinder. The old King was ill, and though all the doctors in the land had tried, none could heal him.

So they called in a magician, who declared that the King could be cured only by the touch of the Dredaine bird, which lived in a golden cage.

'Where can one find this bird?' asked the King.

'In the castle of the Princess Marcassa, which is beyond the Sea of Blood, surrounded by three towering walls, with three courtyards guarded by three tall giants, and with dragons who breathe fire for seven leagues all about the castle.' answered the magician.

The King smiled a royal smile and asked, 'Who will fetch me the Dredaine bird from this terrible castle?'

'I will, father,' shouted the eldest son, and taking gold and silver, and the best mount in the stables, he set out immediately. 'If I do not return in a year and a day, then know that I am dead,' he yelled manfully as he rode out through the gate. Everyone cheered him, and several young girls blushed and fainted.

He rode and rode and rode, until he reached England, a terrible place full of ignorant Saxons. He asked everyone he met where he might find the castle of the Princess Marcassa, and the golden cage of the Dredaine bird, but they nodded their heads and laughed behind their hands and did not answer. Finally, he stopped at one of the inns, and what with the warm beer and the plump girls and the drinking companions, he became quite English and forgot what he was supposed to be doing.

After a year and a day the second son asked his father the King if he could go to find the Dredaine bird, as his older brother had clearly failed. He took even more gold and silver, and two horses, and all the girls wept and gave him scarves and garters to carry as love tokens. But when he reached England, he looked around for his brother instead of the castle, and joined him at the inn, where he settled in comfortably to carousing and wenching. He gave all the fine scarves and Breton lace garters to the English girls, who had never seen anything except scratchy, rough, thick woollen clothes before.

After a year and a day Luduenn got up from among the cinders, and saw that his father's illness had become worse with every passing day. He asked if he could go on the quest for a cure.

'Must you go also, my son?' murmured the aged King. 'Why not stay here to close my eyes in death, for if your two strong, manly, handsome brothers have failed, how can you expect to succeed?'

Luduenn asked again and again if he could seek out the palace and the Dredaine bird, until at last his father sighed and said he could go. He was allowed only a small amount of money and was forbidden to take a horse. So he went to the stables and found an ugly dromedary that no one had ever tried to ride before, as it looked so ridiculous and bubbled and hissed and spat at the grooms. But this clumsy creature could gallop seven leagues in one hour, so he made a good choice out of necessity.

When he reached England, he travelled through the towns asking for the castle and the Dredaine bird. At last he came to a place where the women wore scarves and lace, and they told him that the only people who knew about this bird were two drunken foreign princes, who could be found snoring in the pigsty of the inn, where they had been living since they ran out of cash. Luduenn was overjoyed to see his brothers again, and did not mind in the least when they took all his money but for one six-franc coin, and staggered back into the inn, shouting for beer in that peculiar neighing accent that the English have.

Then he became sad at the way they treated him and, leaping on to his dromedary, rode as far as he could from that place. By nightfall he was in a great forest, filled with the cries of wild creatures from the deep shadows all around the path. Luduenn climbed a tree and saw a faint light shining in the distance. It came from a crude hut made of branches, thatched with coarse hay. When he reached the hut a tiny old woman came out and he asked her for lodging for the night.

'No, no,' she said. 'I cannot offer you hospitality, for I have no bed for a guest.'

'Don't worry, Grandmother, for I'm used to sleeping in the cinders on the hearthstone. That will do me fine.'

'Well, I feel sorry for you out in the forest at night, so you'd better come in,' she muttered, though she still seemed reluctant. Luduenn tied his dromedary, fed and watered it for the night, and went into the little hut.

'What is that bad smell, Grandmother?' he asked, with his hand over his nose.

'Oh, that is just my poor old husband. He's eight days dead and still here. No money to bury him, you see, and the priest will not do something for nothing.'

'How much will the burial cost, Grandmother?'

'Oh, a lot of money, more than I've ever seen in my life. Six francs and not a sou less.'

So the next morning Luduenn went the priest and gave him his last coin, the six-franc piece.

'Bury the poor widow's husband straight away,' he said, and when it was done Luduenn and the old woman were the only mourners.

From the forest he rode out on to a wide, dry plain where nothing grew and no rain fell. As he crossed this desert, he realized that a white fox followed him. And at the very end of the desert, the fox ran right up to him and spoke, saying, 'Are you looking for the Dredaine bird?'

'Yes, in truth I am, little fox.'

'The one in the golden cage at the castle of the Princess Marcassa?'

'Yes, the very same. Can you tell me where it is?'

'Not far. Not far. Look up to that high mountain. Can you see the castle on its summit? Well, that is where the bird is, and this is what you must do to win it. The castle is entered through three courtyards with high walls. The first is filled with snakes and toads and venomous reptiles. The second has only snakes, but they share it with vicious tigers. The third has snakes too, but mainly towering giants who defy all entry to the castle.'

'But how can I get in through such guardians, little fox?'

'Not easily, for they stay awake night and day, but they do all sleep deeply for one hour between eleven in the morning and midday, until the last chime of the twelfth hour. You will see them then with their tongues hanging out, and the giants snoring, stretched out on the courtyard floors. You may pass through the three courts, you may even step on the guardians as they sleep and they will not awaken. But you must be through before the last chime of midday, for they awaken then at once.'

'Where do I go once in the castle, little fox?'

'You will find three beautiful chambers there, and I will not tell you what is in them, only that you must pass through them without stopping once. In the fourth chamber you will find the Dredaine bird, sleeping in a golden cage hanging from the roof by three golden chains. Look for a sword that hangs from a golden nail in the wall. Snatch the sword, cut the three golden chains and take the bird in its cage. But you must remember to do all of this before the last chime of midday, or the doors will shut you in and you will never return.

'Thank you, little fox,' said Luduenn and, bracing himself for the ordeal, set off up the mountain.

He arrived at the stroke of eleven, and the first courtyard door was open. As he crossed the first threshold, he walked through giant snakes and ugly reptiles, all asleep. The second courtyard was even worse, for the tigers breath stank of blood, and in the third courtyard the giants' snoring breath suffocated him and made him sick. But Luduenn passed through into the first room safely, as the fox had bidden him.

All that was in the first room was a table with a loaf of bread on it, and as he passed through he tore off a piece and ate it. To his surprise the loaf remained whole when it was torn, so he put it in his pouch for the journey home. In the second room there was nothing but a table with a jug of wine upon it and a glass beside it. He drank a glass of wine, and when he saw that the jug remained full, he drank two more. So he put the jug in his pouch with the bread for the journey home.

In the third room he found a princess, as beautiful as the light of day, in a deep sleep upon a purple bed. He took his shoes off to tiptoe past her and, as the wine had made him bold, he kissed her on his way through. But he remembered the fox's instructions and went on into the fourth room without stopping.

At last he saw the Dredaine bird, asleep in its golden cage hanging from three golden chains. He saw the sword hanging from its golden nail in the wall, and written on the blade were the words: 'I am the sharpest of all. Whoever owns me can kill ten thousand with my fine edge, and cut whatsoever he wills with my blunt edge.'

'Formidable,' said Luduenn and, taking up the sword, he used the blunt edge, which was finer than a hair, and with three cuts cut through the three golden chains. He took the bird, cage, sword and all, and ran back through the three courtyards as midday began to chime. He ran over the giants, tigers and snakes, and leaped on to his dromedary, riding off with the speed of a whirlwind at the stroke of twelve.

When the Princess, the giants, the tigers and the snakes all awakened, they saw that the bird was gone. The snakes breathed out fire and the giants ran after the thief. The flames singed the hair on the back of Luduenn's neck, and on the rump of his dromedary, but the white fox appeared and ran in front, lending them speed and guiding them on. When they crossed the boundary of the power of the Golden Castle, they could not be touched. The white fox disappeared and Luduenn travelled on in peace.

When he had crossed the dry desolation of the plain, he came at last to a roadside inn. Although he ordered the best food in the place, he found it poor, and the bread tasted like sawdust. So Luduenn called for the owner and said, 'This bread is bad.'

'Not all, sir, it is the best in the land, and what is more, the King himself eats this bread.'

So Luduenn pulled the crust from the castle out of his pouch and cut a piece for the innkeeper.

'Tell me,' he said, 'what you think of this bread.'

'It is delicious, delightful. Give me some more of this wonderful bread.'

Luduenn cut another piece and showed the innkeeper that his original crust did not grow smaller with the cutting.

'Where can I get bread like this?'

'You cannot, for this is the only fragment in the world.'

'Sell it to me,' said the innkeeper, 'and I will give you one hundred gold coins for it.'

'Very well, I'll accept the hundred on one condition. You must swear to give the original crust back to the Princess Marcassa of the Golden Castle, if she ever comes looking for it.'

The landlord agreed, for he was sure that no princess would ever come his way to claim a crust of bread.

Luduenn rode on, and that evening he stopped at another inn, where even the best wine seemed sour. And he sold the magic jug of wine to the innkeeper for two hundred pieces of gold, and an oath that he would give the jug back to the princess should she ever come looking for it.

The next he began his long journey to England, where all the people walk straight into their houses with their muddy boots on. He looked for the inn where he had left his two older brothers, but when he arrived he heard bad news. When the last of the money ran out, his brothers had turned to robbing. Now they were in prison, awaiting the death sentence. But the English King was involved in a devastating war with the Emperor of Russia, and was losing the war, so he had forgotten about the prisoners.

Luduenn went straight to the palace to offer his assistance, and although the porter at the gate tried to stop him, he drew the magical sword an inch out of its scabbard and was soon allowed in. When he heard about the power of the sword, the King agreed to have Luduenn fight the Russians in exchange for his brothers' pardon, and the Princes were set free. And when Luduenn marched at the head of the army, the Russians fled at the sight of the sword and he won a great victory.

When he returned to the inn where his brothers were lodged, he found that they owed money to everyone. So Luduenn sold his sword to the innkeeper for settlement of all the debts, and an oath that the sword would be returned to the princess if she came to ask for it.

At last the three brothers began the long journey home, carrying the Dredaine bird in its golden cage. But the older brothers were jealous and they threw Luduenn down a deep well and rode off on his dromedary, thinking to keep the bird for themselves.

When they arrived at their father's court they took all the credit for finding the bird and feasts were held in their honour. But the Dredaine bird, far from curing the ailing old King, became morose and, whenever it was taken near his bed, cried out in rage, becoming so savage that no one could touch it. The King weakened a little each day and was near to death.

Luduenn, meanwhile, was in the well. He floundered in the water, until he saw a white tail lengthening down towards him. It was the tail of the white fox, who pulled him out.

'Go back home,' said the fox, 'and on the way you will meet an aged beggar. Give him every penny that you have and swap clothes with him. And when you reach your father's palace in your rags, ask for any work, however humble. Do not fear, for all is going well, though you may not think so. Those malcontents will be punished as they deserve.'

Luduenn thanked the fox, then asked why he helped him so.

'Do you remember,' the fox asked him, 'that you stayed one night with a rotting corpse and a widow who could not afford a funeral? And you paid the priest with the last of your money, for the burial service?'

'Yes, indeed, my memory of it is clear.'

'Well, I am the soul of that man, the same that you paid to bury. Now I have fulfilled my debt, and you shall not see me again in this world.' And with these words the fox disappeared.

Soon after that Luduenn met with the beggar, just as the fox had predicted. He changed clothes with the beggar and gave him all his money, and then he walked for many days to his father's palace. No one recognized him at first and he was set to feed the pigs. And the pigs did so well and grew so fat that he was set to groom the horses. And the horses became plump and glossy and full of vigour, until the old King began to speak well of the new stableboy.

The two older brothers grew jealous and knew then who the beggar boy was. They looked for a way of discrediting him, and suggested to their father that he would be the ideal servant to feed the Dredaine bird, which bit everyone who came near it. When it saw Luduenn it beat its wings and sang joyfully. He took it upon his finger, and carried it into the King's bedroom. When he heard its song, the King began to recover. But to be fully cured, he decided, he must also make love to the Princess Marcassa, the owner of the bird.

Back at the Golden Castle the Princess had given birth to a son nine months after Luduenn had kissed her. This little boy soon began to talk, and asked about his father. She answered that she did not know who his father might be.

'We must go to find him,' said the boy. 'I shall not rest until I know who he is.' And so they set out, crossing the dry plain and coming into the world of human habitation. They stopped at an inn to rest, and when they were served the magical bread, they knew that the boy's father had travelled this way.

'You must give me that bread,' said the Princess to the innkeeper.

'Not to anyone in the wide world, no one but the Princess from the Golden Castle can have this bread,' he replied.

'Silly man, I am the Princess from the Golden Castle, it's my bread, and I'm taking it with me.' So into her purse it went. And because the innkeeper had already become rich by the magical bread, and because he knew that only the true Princess would be so rude, he let it go as he had promised. The same happened at the second inn with the magic jug of wine, and at the third with the sword.

'We're close to your father now,' said the Princess, 'for we have all three – bread, wine and sword.' And they travelled on until they reached Paris, where she had her presence formally announced at the palace.

The old King was overjoyed that she had come and, even though he was still ailing, he went out to help her down from her golden carriage.

'I will come down only for the man who took the Dredaine bird from my palace,' she said haughtily.

'That's me, I am the one,' said the eldest son, who had put on his best red robe and cleaned his teeth with a twig.

'If you are he,' she replied, 'tell me how my castle is protected.' He thought for a while, and said that it had very high walls, which was a good guess but the wrong one.

'You are not he. Depart.' No sooner had she said this than the second son leapt forward, and he had new boots on and had rubbed fresh hogs' grease into his hair.

'I cannot keep it a secret any longer,' he said, smiling. 'It was I who took the bird.'

'So how is my castle guarded?' But he had no better answer than his big brother, and she sent him packing, saying, 'If the man who stole the Dredaine bird is not here, then I shall leave and never return.' So Luduenn came out, in his dirty stable clothes, and said, 'I am the man. Your castle has three high walls and three courtyards. In the first are poisonous snakes and reptiles, in the second there are fewer snakes but in the company of lions and tigers. In the third courtyard are more snakes, with enormous giants, and the snakes are like dragons, for they spew fire and flames and burning smoke for seven leagues around.' And he bent his head to show her a burn mark on his neck.

'Well, you know something more than the other two did, but anyone could have told you that. Tell me more,' said the Princess.

'All the guardians sleep from eleven in the morning until midday, and that is how I passed through. In the first room I found the magic bread. In the second the magic jug of wine. But the third room held a lovely princess asleep on a gold and purple bed.'

'And what did you do when you saw her?' asked the Princess softly.

'I looked upon her beauty with astonishment, my mouth hanging open. Then, being bold with the wine, I took my shoes off, lay on the bed and gave her a kiss.'

'That is the truth,' said the Princess. 'And here is your son to prove it . . . But carry on with your story.'

'In the fourth room I used the sword to cut the golden chains that held the cage of the Dredaine bird. And with birdcage, sword, wine and bread, I fled at the stroke of twelve.'

'And where are these wonders now?' asked the Princess.

'The bird is here, but I left the bread, wine and sword at three inns along the way.'

'And I have reclaimed them and brought them here. Now bring me the bird. I must see it at once.' So Luduenn brought the golden cage and bird was in it. When it saw the Princess, it sang loudly for joy and beat its wings, and everyone in the palace heard it and was happy, except the two older brothers.

The Princess took the bird on to her finger and told the old King to stroke it gently. And as soon as he touched it, he was cured. Next she told him of the cruelty and folly of his two older sons, and how in the end they had tried to murder their little brother.

The king shouted aloud, 'Let them be cast into a hot oven', and so they were.

Not long after that, Luduenn married the Princess Marcassa, and they had such a vast, lavish wedding feast that the old King died from overeating. And Luduenn became king in his place.

From Breton oral tradition, collected and published by F. M. Luzel in
Contes Populaires de Basse-Bretagne, Paris, 1879
(English version by R. J. Stewart)

SONG OF THE WIND

Unriddle me this, if you can
I was before God's flood
without flesh or vein or bone
headless, footlessly I stride
nothing's child, never born
when my breath stills, I am not dead
no older now, nor ever young
I have no need of beast or man

sea-whitener, forest-piercer
handless I touch a whole field
Time's partner, Youth's partaker
wide as the wide earth is wide
unequalled, masterless, never prisoner
landless, invisible and blind
solitary and brash of manner
gentle, murderous, and without sin
I am no repairer of disorder
I am wet and dry and weak and strong
what am I? that the cold moon fosters
and the ardour of the sun.

From Welsh tradition, attributed to Taliesin
(English version by Robin Williamson)

LAMMAS

summer of kisses, summer unlasting
to walk all never and now
of the ermine darkness
between hills till all tangles rest
in love and alone
through the vowing harvest

once of a summer it was the fine of scythes
to hear the hour bells chime 13
with a cherish of ghosts through the eel grass
into the dark
was the running of horses to their wings
into the dark
un-nails the crucifix

summer of parks and prams
cobble my step through the trades of silence
where mongerers' clocky streets in shadow lean
where under the biscuit eaves
sleep the toothless and the fanged together
where church yards measure the dead
their separate grin

summer without cunning
I cast the three threads of sorrow
gaffed out with the goat's vane
the night the cuckoos cease to sing
for all the dapple girls
I'll never catch or lose at all
o the dark is full of wanton chirps
and adder's climb

summer it is late and early
and the bride of the old old story
gives clasp and key to lovers now
in the break of a finger's end
between the stood stalk and the fatal sheaf
a match flare once in each other's eyes
it's then the dark legend
out-whites the moon

summer of simple truths
our arms are about the moonlight
children in their quilt palaces festooned
already hear
the hare of the brown mountains
thump in their heedless loins
of the wrinkle of apples
and the snow to come

summer of stubblefires and hemlocks
I'll stare from the low ground
till the stars twisting come in heaven's pool
till the dragon slayer loose
the king's daughter that prophesies of autumn
and to the human song
the sisters beside the well

summer of wireless and canaries
I have sold my mouth to the song
to hack after the angelic language
in the written world
loving the two of magpies
and the authority of the weather
loving most what cannot be seen
or said at all

summer of those
who will pass this way after me.

Robin Williamson

Here ends the Second Part, That of The Sacred Head – Wisdom
Through Suffering – The Sacred King and Poet

PART THREE

RETURN TO THE SOURCE
◆
WISDOM THROUGH INSPIRATION
◆
THE LIGHT WITHIN

INTRODUCTION

Robin Williamson

approach every part of Celtic tradition – music, story, riddle and reel, from the deepest, darkest ballad to the simplest children's rhyme – in the belief that it contains truth and teaching.

It takes years of telling to grasp the full import of any fairy-story, and in a way the story has to find you first. Stories bring luck on those who tell them and on those who hear them. What is luck? One who is lucky gets a helping hand from the unseen; honesty, generosity and kindness bring luck, while pride and greed hinder it. This is illustrated in the following Scottish story, which I learned from my friend and honorary uncle, the great traveller story-teller Duncan Williamson. There's a teaching in this story and there's plenty of politicians would be better for learning it.

◆

JACK AND THE THREE BANISHED ELVES

JACK WAS ALWAYS hungry, never could get his fill. One day he was sitting on his steps, with his feet in the gutter. He was thinking, 'Christ, if I only had a sausage, a slice of bread – just a crust of bread would do fine. He felt a tapping on his ankle. Three elves were standing there – striped hats, pointy shoes, the lot.

'We're elves,' they said

'Right,' said Jack. 'Why aren't you in Elfland?'

'We're banished. The King's gold's been stolen. He thinks we did it. You can help us, though, and if you do, you'll get a plate that's never cleared, a cup that's never empty. Besides, in Elfland you get three courses every meal, three meals every day.'

'Three courses! Three meals! I'll never get through the door, I'm too big. And where is it?'

'No problem.' The elves all waved their hands. Jack became the same size as them and with the suit.

'Round the corner, that's where the door is.'

Off he went round the corner. And sure enough there were the gates of Elfland, 300 miles high, made out of boiling cascades of molten metals and *diamanté* sparkle, with wee imps jumping in and out shouting, 'One drop more won't hurt you.' Jack rang the bell like you would and walked into Elfland, straight into the dining room, sat down at the table, said to the elf next to him, 'How many courses do we get for dinner again?'

'Three courses every meal.'

At that moment in walked a cook with a huge pot of soup. Jack leapt to his feet, shouting, 'This is the first', and the cook put the soup

Page 112: *The story-teller with his* crwth

down and looked at Jack queerly. He went back to the kitchen in a hurry. He said to the other cook, 'There's an elf in there that looked right at me and said, "This is the first." How could he know.'

'He knows nothing,' said the other. 'Wait you till I go in with the meat.' He put the big leg of lamb on the silver plate and in he went with it. Jack was waving his hands in the air, saying 'This is the second.' Cook went ashen, ran back to the kitchen. 'You're right. He knows.'

'No, no, no,' says the third cook. 'How could he know we took it? Wait you till I've gone in with the pudding.' He put the jam roll out with the custard. In he went.

'This is the third,' roared Jack.

The cook put the pudding down very carefully on the table and he whispered in Jack's ear, 'Don't tell the King. We'll put the gold back. It'll be as if it was never one.'

And that was how Jack got the wee magic cup and the wee magic plate. And I should get a wee half-gill of whisky for telling you all these lies.

Traditional
(This version by Robin Williamson)

———————— ◆ ————————

In many stories there is a clear direction to be true to oneself, to honestly seek one's heart's desire.

It is true that music is a teacher because it comes from Annwn and goes to Gwnwyd, because it passes the brain by and talks to the soul.

It is true that contentment is wealth. The best education is to be found in the tradition together with sexual true love, children and journeying.

The saying of St Cynog: 'Half of the learning is already in the head.'

In trying to teach somebody something, the primary problem is to convince them that they do not already know it. This applies particularly to an art involving a skill, as illustrated in the following story from South Wales.

THE LORD OF CARDIFF'S JUMP

THE LORD OF CARDIFF decided he would give a great feast to the noblemen of Britain. The feast was to celebrate his many achievements. But for every boast the Lord of Cardiff could make, someone would rise with a claim to have bettered his achievement, doubled it or excelled it beyond comparison. Finally, in exasperation he said, 'You may have observed my fine tower here. Many reckon it is one of the tallest, if not the tallest, tower in the whole of Britain. Yet I can jump to the top of it.'

There were, of course, murmurs of disbelief. A demonstration was demanded. The nobles followed the Lord of Cardiff to the foot of his tower.

The Lord of Cardiff placed his knees and his ankles together, drew a deep breath and jumped . . . to the first step and then to the second, and so to the top of the tower.

Shouts were heard to the tune of 'Anyone could have done that.'

'Certainly they could,' replied the Lord of Cardiff, 'had they had the wit to grasp the jest.'

Traditional
(This version by Robin Williamson)

A Bit More History

The Roman imperialists with their armies and their slavery were defused by the very story they sought to employ politically, by the Christian story of the wonderful child, of the wonderful mother, of his inspired life and of his mystical death and rebirth. The druids already knew this story very well. Druids became priests of the Celtic Christian Church during the Roman occupation of Britain in the first four centuries AD, wonder-workers as ever but now called saints.

Throughout the Middle Ages the harper, the poet and the scholar were honoured in Wales, Scotland and Ireland. Under the Tudor kings and queens, Welsh matters were rather in vogue, as the monarchy was of Welsh ancestry. The story of Prince Madog and his legendary discovery of America was promoted under Elizabeth I as evidence of rights in Virginia and America at large.

The Welsh harp as well as the Irish harp found favour at the court of James I and throughout the bloody years of the Civil War, rampant Puritanism notwithstanding, harp music remained in favour. 'No great house in England,' says John Aubrey in his *Brief Lives*, 'did not in my boyhood fail to boast of a resident harper.'

Interest flourished in Arthurian material after Malory's *Morte d'Arthur* and finally, just as the last of the Gaelic-language poets of Scotland and Ireland were dwindling to beggary, comes the rise of Celtic music in the New World.

In these days comes the brilliant voice of Edward Williams.

Iolo Morgannwg

Edward Williams, best known by his bardic name, Iolo Morgannwg, was born in Llancarfan, near Cardiff, in 1747. As he was a weak child he received no formal education, but learned his alphabet from tombstone inscriptions cut by his father who was a stone mason. He learned reading, writing and something of music from his mother and from his earliest years he displayed a love of history. It was noted he had a very retentive memory.

Iolo went to London in 1770, after the death of his mother, and there he formed friendships with other enthusiasts for the ancient history of Britain and for Welsh literature and its revival. Due to his connections in London, it is not impossible that in his later years he may have met and possibly influenced William Blake, who was 20 years his junior.

He returned to Wales in 1777, residing in Flemington, near Cowbridge. In the final years of his life, he published two key works in the bardic revival, the *Myrvyrian Archaiology of Wales* in 1801 and the famous *Barddas*. He died in 1826, aged 81, and was buried in Flemington.

From individual country houses in Wales he gathered together manuscript material which related to the entire legacy of bardic thought and druidry. He collected, translated and caused to be published the *Triads of the Island of Britain*. Iolo Morgannwg is the father of the modern Eisteddfod in Wales and of the revival druid movement, which flourishes now in both English- and Welsh-speaking Britain with much variety: revival druidry actually has members ranging from bikers to bankers.

The so-called Celtic Twilight authors of early-twentieth-century Scotland and Ireland have ushered in what has been a major reflowering of Celtic art throughout the world, together with a new dawn of respect for the older mysteries. This has not only made its mark in the obvious fields of ecological awareness, animal rights and women's and men's movements, but is also in the forefront of modern science, for in the fields of astrophysics, computer research and chaos theory a paradoxical similarity to profundities long ago voiced in bardic philosophy is observable.

The harder one looks, the more one sees. The pattern interlocks and repeats between the part and the whole. Better observation leads to greater appreciation of the vast mystery in which we have our being in a way that would have been unthinkable in Victorian science, which seemed to have everything sewn up.

Has it at last become acceptable for society to re-create the sanctity of the natural world, the spirit in earth? So much evil has been done in the name of religion. The race defines God, the unknowable, in ways that are mentally graspable. How often this has made God monstrous. In many ways the forest may be a better and truer temple for the future than any church. The hillside spring. Day dawns.

THE FACE OF THE SUN

The three extraordinary works of the Island of Britain:
The ship of Nwydd Nav Neivion which brought the first living
   things when the lake of floods burst forth
The stone of Gwyddon Ganhebon upon which the arts and
   sciences of the world were carved
And the oxen of Hu Gadarn that drew the *afanc* from the lake of
   floods, so that the lake of floods burst forth no more.

The three primary inventors of the Island of Britain:
Tydain, father of poetic genius, who taught the secret of poetry
   and the memorization of song
Dynwall Moelmud, who taught the first laws of Britain with their
   privileges and customs
And Hu Gadarn, who was the first warrior chieftain of hosts.

The three first makers of song in the Island of Britain:
Tydain, father of poetry
Gwyddon Ganhebon, who sang the first song in the world
And Hu Gadarn, who taught song as the memorization of
   knowledge.

From Welsh tradition
(English version by Robin Williamson)

These 'Triads' encapsulate the traditional lore of the Hu Gadarn. Nineteenth-century druidry viewed Hu Gadarn as a title of the sun in the height of its progress through the year. Other solar titles of the sun in its full strength were Lleu, Taliesin and Arthur. The nineteenth-century revival bard Morien O Morgan envisaged the annual progress of the sun about his native area around Pontypridd. Remember that in his day Pontypridd and the Welsh valleys in general were experiencing the full, dark satanic coal boom. A central part of his vision, and vision it was, as the notion of the Ark. This he related to the megalithic stone on Pontypridd Common, known as the Pontypridd Rocking Stone, which was the physical representation of the magical Ark which would carry the sun under the sea in the midwinter solstice to his rebirth again as the crowned babe.

The dark midwinter is the focus for the highly complex interlace of bardic ideas shallowly submerged in the four branches of the *Mabinogion*, and the '*Triads of the Island of Britain*.' These relate to the notion of the imprisoned sun.

The Great Prisoner

The three great prisoners of the Island of Britain:
Llyr Llediaith, father of Bran the Blessed
Madwg or Mabon, son of Medrawg or Modron
Gair or Gwair, son of Geirion.

The release of Mabon by Arthur is related in the story 'Culhwch and Olwen' (see pages 58–69), while the release of Gwalr by Arthur is implied in 'The Spoils of Annwn' (see pages 42–47).

The name of Gwair's father, Geirion, derives apparently from the early Celtic Tigernonus, meaning great king. His mother would therefore be the great of Rigantona, a prototype of Rhiannon in the *Mabinogion*. Gwair's story must be affiliated, then, with the story of Rhiannon's child Pryderi.

Mabon, Gwair or Pryderi would be poetic names for the imprisoned not yet risen, sun. The traditional name of the prison is Caer Oeth and Anoeth, the dark prison under stone. This is said to have been made by Manawydan, the son of the sea, out of human bones.

The prison-of-bones idea relates to another large interlace of bardic ideas about the great prisoner. This has to do with the imprisonment of the soul in the body. The lore relates to the freeing of the prisoner spirit in man via inspiration from Awen.

There is throughout the Celtic material a linking of the soul to the progress of the seasons, to the progress of the sun and of the moon. Stone circles and stone avenues mark these respectively. Aspirant bards appear to have walked with a teacher through significant sites of sacred landscape as part of their training. Such sacred landscapes have existed in many parts of Britain since ancient times, but a magical landscape can be envisaged anywhere. William Blake managed in the streets of London.

The Mabon

The Mabon, meaning lad or son, figures in the four branches of the *Mabinogion* (the lad's stories). In branch one and three he is called Pryderi, child of Pwll and Rhiannon. In branch two he is called Gwern, child of Branwen and Matholwch. And in branch four he is called Lleu Llaw Gyffes, child of Arianrhod.

Careful study of the *Mabinogion* will produce glimmerings of insight into earlier lost Celtic ideas of the wonderful child. Scarcely to be remarked on is the recurrent heretical tendency in medieval Britain to refer to Arthur as Christ. Arthur was the name to last the longest as the youngest of the Celtic gods or faces of the sun, and his name is of course in common parlance to this day: 'His deeds better than meat to those who will recite his praises.'

Radicalism, prophecy and conscience

Celtic tales make mention of an inspired bard delivering prophecy in a state compared to madness. In *Phaedo* the Greek philosopher Socrates says, 'Greatest blessings come by way of madness, provided it is inspired by a god.' He differentiates between prophetic madness inspired by Apollo, ritual madness inspired by Dionysus, poetic madness inspired by the nine Muses and erotic madness inspired by Aphrodite. All deities have their counterparts in the British pantheon.

Bards used to deliver inspired judgements in legal cases in early Ireland. These proved so difficult to interpret that trial by ordeal was invented, and finally the ordeal of the modern legal system. The classic tale of prophecy in the British tradition is the one that follows below.

◆

THE FIRST PROPHECY OF MERLIN

LONG AND AGO and before the days of Arthur, Vortigern, Earl of Gwent, made himself king of treachery and murder. In his need for armed warriors, he hired Saxon mercenaries. And in his lust for the beautiful daughter of Hengist, the Saxon king, Vortigern committed the prime error of Celtic history. He gave land to the Saxons. It was to be in exchange for one night with Rowena. That was the daughter's name. Vortigern was drunk when he made this arrangement and for this reason he is remembered as one of the three disgraceful drunkards of the island of Britain.

The island of Thanet was the land he gave them. Thanet in the Thames. But the Saxons stopped not there. They captured London, York, Lincoln, Winchester, slaying as wolves slay sheep unshepherded. And Vortigern fled before them into Wales.

There he took counsel with his chief wizards. And they gave him prime advice: to build a stronghold. Upon Mount Snowdon was the favoured site, the highest peak in the land. But whatever the King's masons built by day was swallowed into the earth by night. His wizards counselled him further, saying nothing would hold the stones firm but the blood of a boy who had never had a father.

So search was made and such a boy was found, in the town now called Carmarthen, where a lady of noble birth, and a nun moreover, had conceived a child to a spirit of the air. For as learned Apuleius reports, 'Certain spirits between the earth and moon partake of the nature of both men and angels.' Surely such a spirit had fathered the boy they brought to Vortigern. Merlin was his name.

No word or gesture betrayed the boy as sentence of death was read to him, and his blood required of him to firm the stones. But he said, 'Bid your wizards come forward and I will reveal their ignorance to you, O King.'

They were brought at once for the boy spoke with power. He inquired of the wizards, 'Since you claim knowledge, what lies below these foundations?'

The wizards were abashed and answered not a word.

'Bid your workmen dig deeper, O King, and they will pierce to the waters of a great pool.'

They did. And so it was. Waters filled all the land about.

'Drain these,' said Merlin. 'You will find two huge stones and in them, asleep, one red dragon and one white.'

They did. And so it was. And the dragons awoke, flapped ponderously into the skies and there attacked each other, fire and claw, the white dragon and the red.

Then Merlin drew in the breath of prophecy, and spoke these words as the bards relate:

alas, alas the red dragon
for the hour of his doom is rung
for the red is our own portent
as the white is the Saxons'
and they will be our affliction
sore and long
our hills they will lay waste and our mountains
our valleys' streams will course with blood
churches of our faith razed and ruined
still will be the worship of our God.
Until the wild boar bears the crown from Cornwall
to rule the ocean's islands and the forests of Gaul
till even the house of Romulus will tremble
his last fate no seer will foretell
his name will be the fame of all his people
his deeds better than meat to those who will recite his praise.

From Geoffrey of Monmouth, *Historia Regum Britanniae*
(This version by Robin Williamson)

It is clear that this excerpt from Merlin's lengthy prophecy foretells the coming of Arthur.

We usually tend to think of prophesy in this sense of prediction, a breath of inspiration indrawn, a foretelling of events to come, especially in imagistic language similar to the so-called speaking in tongues.

In our century, having solved none of the fundamental human problems relating to the extraordinary fact of being alive, the modern artist often has more to do with the notion of prophecy as a revelation of the present, a vision of the greater reality of what is, and the poet/artist of the last 200 years has increasingly spoken as a conscience of the people.

The present Celtic vision has a radical political as well as a mystical bent. In this context, I would like to make further note of the primary English bard, bard in the full sense, William Blake. In the following extract he has this to say on the subject of the 'reasonable' politics of greed with which he was – and we are still – surrounded, the spirit of industrial manipulation which he called Urizen.

URZIEN READ IN HIS BOOK OF BRASS

Compel the poor to live upon a crust of bread, by soft mild arts.
Smile when they frown, frown when they smile; & when a man
  looks pale
With labour & abstinence, say he looks healthy and happy;
And when his children sicken, let them die; there are enough
Born, even too many, & our Earth will be overrun
Without these arts. If you would make the poor live with temper
With pomp give every crust of bread you give; with gracious
  cunning
Magnify small gifts; reduce the man to want a gift, & then give
  with pomp.
Say he smiles if you hear him sigh. If pale, say he is ruddy.
Preach temperance; say he is overgorg'd & drowns his wit
In strong drink, tho' you know that bread and water are all
He can afford. Flatter his wife, pity his children, till we can
Reduce all to our will, as spaniels are taught with art.

Think again about Taliesin, the bright son of Ceridwen and dark, winged Afagddu, her other son, and consider this further excerpt from the works of Blake:

> A Vegetated Christ and a Virgin Eve
> are the Hermaphroditic Blasphemy
> By his Maternal Birth he is that Evil One
> And his Maternal Humanity
> must be put off Eternally
> Lest the sexual Generation
> swallow up Regeneration
> Come Lord Jesus,
> take on thee the Satanic Body of Holiness.

There's something important being said here about the light and dark; about the error of ascetic reason, which seeks to separate spirit from earth, the earth from the spirit.

Cattwg the Wise

There are a number of fables attributed to Cattwg the Wise, the fifth–sixth-century-AD Abbot of Llancarfan, who would take his retreats on the island of Steep Holm, there conversing with the sea-gulls and keeping an eye upon the spire of Glastonbury, of which he was also abbot, some say. Cattwg was a Christian saint and a bard.

◆

THE FOWLER AND THE COOPER

A fowler and a cooper went out into the wood together, one to snare birds, one to seek sticks for barrel hoops. They walked carefully and slowly, searching diligently among the groves.

'There,' whispered the fowler. 'Look, a woodcock.'

'Where?' said the cooper.

'There, by the foot of that alder bush,' said the fowler.

'Is it near that likely clump of barrel-hoop sticks? said the cooper.

'Barrel hoop, barrel hoop. What do you mean? It's by that hazel tree now.'

'I don't know what a hazel tree looks like.'

'Well, I don't know what a likely-looking barrel-hoop stick looks like.'

Traditional
(This version by Robin Williamson)

◆

So in this world people seek what they wish to find and they easily find that. Things for which they care nothing remain invisible to them, be they never so obvious.

> The three first parts of all understanding:
> An eye to see what is
> A heart to feel what is
> And a boldness that dares follow them.

One who wishes, then, their life to be an adventure, beginning once upon a time and ending lived happily ever after, one who has the head and the heart for it, has the makings of a bard. But in addition to everything the 'Triads' have to say, the tales add this between the lines: 'Practise the conquest of one's own vanity and egotism, watch how the world wags, be kind and respectful to others and luck will find you.'

And having said all that:

> *tlws goreu'n bod*
> *yw gwain tafod*

> The best ornament
> is a sheath for the tongue.

BLIND RAFTERY THE POET

OF COURSE WHEN the story starts, he wasn't a poet and he wasn't blind. Raftery was a young fellow then making a bit of a living playing the fiddle: weddings, funerals, other festivities. Death's always been a popular subject for humour where I come from, where in many towns the smoke from the crematorium is the only sign of life. My elderly aunt went to get measured for her coffin and the undertaker said to her, 'Well, Miss McGillivary, I suppose you'll be wanting the white satin lining. Normally the unmarried ladies have the white satin lining and the married ladies have the purple satin lining. So I suppose you'll be wanting the white satin, Miss McGillivary.'

Well, she glared at him and she said, 'I suppose it will need to be the white satin since I was never married, but I'll have five or six purple ribbons to show I wasn't entirely neglected.'

So Raftery, one night or morning was making his way home. He was overtaken by a shower of rain. The only shelter he could find was under a small hazel tree beside the road. Not much shelter, that. The rain was pouring down the back of Raftery's neck. He was drookit as they say in Scotland. He looked up at the tree in exasperation, saying, 'Why could you not have a bit more bush on you? Your twigs are bald.'

Now Raftery had no way of knowing that this hazel tree was one of the original hazel trees, brought over at the time of the great Deluge by the MacPhee himself, who had his own boat at the Flood for he wouldn't go in with Noah. So Raftery was astonished to hear the tree reply, 'You'd be bald yourself if you'd been standing here since the Flood.'

The tree then related to Raftery the entire history of Ireland, starting with Noah's brother, Partholon, and continuing through the entire Book of Invasions, not omitting the Danes or the English. And the tree had got as far as the wart on Oliver Cromwell's nose when Raftery, noting that the rain had ceased, beat a retreat.

But he had something to say for himself then. All that he had heard from the tree. And he got the name as a poet, but he wasn't blind. Not then.

Anyone who's ever tried it will tell you that poetry is thirsty work. Raftery began to lean a little more heavily on the native cordial. So he was coming home about a year later, having a glass taken. It was not so much the length of the road as the breadth of it that was troubling him. His feet and his head were having a disagreement and so he decided he would lie down and let the three of them sort it out between them.

It was the sound of an axe that woke him, the sound of someone chopping wood. Following that sound, he came to a clearing, where stood a small man as broad as he was tall, with a great double-bladed axe in his hand. A short, stocky man, with a pugnacious, red butcher of a face on him, eyebrows like bottle brushes.

He said to Raftery, 'My name is the Jealous Hero. I will not ask your name. But you will follow me now to my house. There you will hear my story.'

Raftery was five feet ten of pure curiosity all his life. So off he went with the Jealous Hero to the Jealous Hero's house. The kind you'd call a but and ben, one room in the front, one room in the back. Raftery sat down beside the Jealous Hero's fire to listen.

THE JEALOUS HERO'S STORY

'When I was younger than I am, I set out into the world to seek for better times and to push my own fortune. I wandered at last into the far north and into the land that is called Siberia. There I found worse times than I had ever found before, for I was overtaken, like Napoleon before me, by the bitter winter. I could feel my strength failing me as I stumbled into the endless whiteness of the snows. I could feel myself sinking into the slumber that is the slumber of eternity.

'It was at that time I heard a voice roaring and shouting. Coming through the air towards me, riding upon a cartwheel which he was rowing with a short oar, was a little man. And by the red hair that was curling from his head to his two heels, I could tell he was that class of a wizard you would call a Gruagach.

'He said to me, "I am the Gruagach here. The Gruagach of the Claddagh Fuar. And I have an enemy and you will kill him for me. As your reward you will wed my daughter."

'I said to him, "Gruagach or not, there's no way I'll kill anyone, for I am myself dying in the snows."

'He said to me, "You have a little trick in your right hand you never knew you had before that will drive a man's brains in fiery flinders out of the backbone of his skull. My daughter is the finest woman in the western world or in the eastern world. Her hair is like the midnight. Her face is like the morning. And you're lucky to be getting the offer of her rather than dying there like a dog in the drifts. Catch a grip of my ankle, lad."

'He whisked me through the air and set me down before the door of his house. Upon the plain of combat before the door where stood the pole of combat, all hung with bones and skulls. The Gruagach gave the pole a kick with his foot until the bones and skulls all rattled on and there issued out of the ground like smoke the enemy of the Gruagach in his powers.

'I greeted him civilly, courteously, with mannerly manly words of high understanding and with the greeting and the gesture called the *fiscne fascne*. And if he answered me back no better, he answered me not a whit the worse. Then with the little trick in my right hand I never knew I had before, I drove the brains of his head in fiery flinders out of the backbone of his skull.

'They married me then to the Gruagach's daughter whose hair was like the midnight, whose face was like the morning. But what with the weight of the feasting table and the depth of the drinking glass, I never got as far as her bed that night.

'If I woke early next morning, my father-in-law was awake before me, shouting and roaring to be out to the hunting hill to hunt foxes and badgers and vermin. In the taking of the game and the laying of it down, it was evening before I got back to the house of my mother-in-law. It was the sound of wailing that greeted me there and I asked her the cause of her sorrow and of her lamentation. "Alas and *ochone*," she said. "The wife that you married but one day past has been taken from you by the Grey Champion."

'I took the evil and the good of that upon myself. I took the track of the duck on the ninth dawn. I put my shoulder against the boat, but the boat was too heavy for me. I put the sinew, the marrow, the blood of my body into that shove. I put her prow to the sea, stern to the shore. No

Gruagach, an otherworld being in Scottish tradition

mast unbent, no sail untorn. I hoisted the tall, tough, speckled sails against the tall, tough, splintery masts. My music was the screeching of gulls and the twisting and splashing of eels. And the beast that was best ate the beast that was least and the beast that was least did as best as it may and the bent brown buckie in the base bones of the sea played Hoig on its mouth all the way to the island of the Grey Champion.

'I drew the ship a ship's length up the beach, that the boys and scholars of the yellow town might not be making scholarly sport and mockery of her. I went into the island.

'There stood the Grey Champion, my wife beside him.

'I greeted him civilly, courteously with mannerly manly words of high understanding and with the greeting and the gesture called the *fiscne fascne*. And if he answered me back no better, he answered me not a whit the worse. Then with the little trick in my right hand I never knew I had before, I drove the brains of his head in fiery flinders out of the backbone of his skull.

'Then I took my wife back.

'But what with the weight of the feasting table and the depth of the drinking glass, I never got as far as her bed that night.

'If I woke early next morning, my father-in-law was awake before me, shouting and roaring to be out to the hunting hill to hunt foxes and badgers and vermin. In he taking of the game and the laying of it down, it was evening before I got back to the house of my mother-in-law. It was the sound of wailing that greeted me there and I asked her the cause of her sorrow and of her lamentation. "Alas and *ochone*," she said. "The wife that you married but two days past has been taken from you by the Hero of the Claive Soleesh, the Hero of the Sword of Light."

'I took the evil and the good of that upon myself. I took the track of the duck on the ninth dawn. I put my shoulder against the boat, but the boat was too heavy for me. I put the sinew, the marrow, the blood of my body into that shove. I put her prow to the sea, stern to the shore. No mast unbent, no sail untorn. I hoisted the tall, tough, speckled sails against the tall, tough, splintery masts. My music was the screeching of gulls and the twisting and splashing of eels. And the beast that was best ate the beast that was least and the beast that was least did as best as it may and the bent brown buckie in the base bones of the sea played Hoig on its mouth all the way to the island of the Hero of the Claive Soleesh.

'There stood the Hero, my wife beside him.

'I greeted him civilly, courteously with mannerly manly words of high understanding and with the greeting and the gesture called the *fiscne fascne*. And if he answered me back no better, he answered me not a whit the worse.

'I was just about to drive the brains of his head in fiery flinders out of the backbone of his skull with the wee trick in my right hand I never knew I had before when the Hero stood on his right leg, closed his right eye, lifted his right hand with the forefinger crooked and placed me under a Geasa, under crosses and under spells, that I would never get one kiss from my wife, nor hear one word from her mouth, until she would get a kiss from Raftery the poet.

'So the question I have to ask you now is, what is your name? For if you are not Raftery the poet, I will drive the brains of . . . '

'Well now,' shouted Raftery. 'There is no need for you to exert yourself, for I am the man you seek.'

So the Jealous Hero brought Raftery then into the back room of his house, where sat the most beautiful of women in the western world or in the eastern world, winding a golden thread upon a silver spindle, passing the time so.

The kiss that Raftery gave her was the kiss that put words back into her mouth. But that same kiss was the kiss that took the sight away from Raftery's eyes.

Or so Raftery might have told the story. For you wouldn't want to ruin a good story by sticking too close to fact.

PLAYING MUSIC TO EMPTY POCKETS

He had the name Blind Raftery the Poet from that time. Blind Raftery the Poet was famous the length and breadth of Ireland. His poems were printed in books. The books were sold in Dublin shops and sold again from barrows in the Ivy Market and the Daisy Market.

The way the world wags, Raftery outlived his fame. He was seated then an old, old man by the roadside near the town of Galway. He was playing the fiddle. A passer-by asked of him his name in the world, as it had been asked of him before in a story.

> And Raftery replied:
> I am blind Raftery the poet
> My gentleness without misery
> Going westward by the light of my heart
> Though weak and tired and at the end of a road
> I am now
> My back against the wall
> Playing music to empty pockets

From the Irish tradition
(This version by Robin Williamson)

◆

MERLIN'S RETURN

ONE NIGHT IN NOVEMBER, when the seven stars of the Pleiades are closely watched and hallowed gates stand ready to open, the prophet Merlin sat awake in his observatory tower. Scattered about him were the implements of his art – a rough fragment of brown stone upon which white crystals grew; a small apple branch twisted into a loop, where the parent tree had grown over a hidden spring; a simple wooden bowl filled with red well water; a hooked sickle of polished golden bronze.

The prophet had watched stars crawl within the layers of night, seeing within the sky-shadows each fold of the Lady's Shawl, each curve and twist of her weaving. He had followed the racing moon as she sped to encompass all nocturnal events before dawn; he had marked where star rays touched upon certain power places, signalling potential futures of mortal men. Yet he felt incomplete.

The night before the hallows were revealed, before the portals opened, yet Merlin felt unready. He could not sense a quality or action required for completion, or discern in which of the four directions it might be found. Below his tower a thick mist rolled about the hilltop, creeping to a shadow daybreak. In one hour the time of inner knowledge would pass him by.

What had he missed? What forgotten? The prophet picked up his apple branch and touched it lightly to the crystalline rock; his awareness reached down, far within the earth below the hill, and he spoke the names of two dragons. But he met only that utter silence which falls upon all kingdoms awaiting dawn.

Putting aside his ritual objects, each charged with power, Merlin took three paces to the east of his circular stone chamber; three to the south. He turned next to face north, taking six paces across the centre of the circle to its northern wall; finally he turned to his left and took three steady paces west. The mist outside thickened and slowly curled and twisted, writhing and rising until it covered the tower, seeping through unprotected deep slit windows built for star-watching by daylight. Finally the prophet faced east once more, and took three paces to the centre of his chamber.

He felt not that the mist was rising, but that the tower was plummeting down into the rocky hill below; it seemed to sink like a stone dropped into a wellshaft. For a moment the stout elm boards beneath his feet seemed ready to fall away and leave him floating. Merlin turned to face north once more, pivoting upon the central point, stamping upon the floor and squinting hard at the rough, unadorned stone wall before him.

At first he saw nothing, heard nothing, only the jagged surfaces and planes of the blue lias stone, cut long ago by craftsmen, shaped and laid to make the tower, a long-familiar pattern of surfaces, lines and shadows in the lamplight. But still seeing nothing, he suddenly heard something.

From beyond the north came a hint of sound, then a certain murmuring. The murmuring grew into droning, and the droning became a growling which swelled suddenly into a roaring , until Merlin realized that knowledge of incompletion and completion awaited him in the north, just beyond the thick wall of his downward-plummeting tower.

Yet, being not only a prophet but a bard and (at one time) a madman, he chose merely to wait and listen to the terrible sound that swelled and rose and expanded out of the wall. In that raging storm he could hear voices calling to one another over great distances, speaking in the tongue of a time and place far beyond his own. Certain voices were filled with pain and fear, others uttered firm, dry, hard commands. The sense of great distance would suddenly snap tight and short, until the crying, screaming, ordering voices were packed close together; they would then disperse and echo down long tunnels, and, as if a tide washed them to and fro, they would suddenly regroup within the eye of the sound-storm and scream at one another through its throbbing violence.

Listening, waiting, the prophet gained his first hint towards completion. This was, he realized at last, a convocation of warriors lost in a terrible conflict, wandering spirits of men killed in a far distant war, distant in time if not in space. Those who died thus, sadly and suddenly, were unable to break free from the shadow world into the worlds of light.

He also realized that this was no mere essay in far-seeing or coincidence of imagination; here was a matter of great import, and the vacuum which he had felt before the sound-storm, his sense of being empty and incomplete, had been a vital forerunner and preparation, a low ebb before strong turning of the tide towards flood.

Yet he remained still, standing, filling his spirit with deep silence to absorb the sound; he awaited a sign to enfold the moment, to direct him. As he stood utterly still, facing north in the centre of the circular chamber, a tiny spider scuttled over his bare feet and ran off into the darkness behind him. She had fallen from a small gap between the dry-laid tight-fitting stones of the northern wall, disturbed by the roaring and the voices. She ran directly to the south, where all was quiet: the sign.

So it was that Merlin raised his arms above his head to summon up and open the secret gateway of the north. There had been times in the wildwood, the cavern, in the ancient places filled with power and terror, which had strengthened him for this task. First, he took the name and form of Bear, strong guardian of the icy northern realms. His shoulders grew broad and slumped forward, his arms massive and heavy; his face grew long and keen, and claws ripped open through his hands and feet. His eyesight dimmed greatly, but his hearing and sense of smell were amplified; a great heart beat soundly in his body and he began to turn and weave in motion, sniffing out each quarter of the circle as he moved.

Dancing the shuffling bear dance he drew the strength, courage and motion of the bear into his hands, then passed it right into the northern wall, sealing it with a shape of power known only to those of the Bear lineage. The prophet then spread his arms out straight at shoulder height, level right and left, lowering them from the upraised position. He turned completely around, moving in the pattern known as the Door, spinning for an instant upon one foot, so fast that he seemed to have two heads. The shape of Bear passed from him, but the power of Door flowed out of him into the northern wall, and he sealed it with a colour of power known only to those who are Doorkeepers.

Merlin lowered his arms from their horizontal position, until both hands pointed down to the chamber floor and to the earth below the tower. His fingers shook and his skin pulsed with the flow of power, reaching far down into the core of the planet; slowly he began to raise his arms again, slowly and greatly laden, bearing a burden of rising force without form. As his rigid trembling hands reached out before him, drawing level with his shoulders, he turned his wrists in the supple undulating pattern of Opening.

As the Opening was born, he uttered an ascending musical call that crept from the depths of earth, low and grinding at first, then crystalline and deep, then swelling waves of ocean and roar of trees meeting wind. Within that call were all the undertones, tones and overtones of music through the three worlds. Suddenly it rose into the heights and twisted into the high triumphant scream of the hawk flying into sunlight in the month of May. And with this sound, known only to those who are Merlin, he sealed the Opening into the northern wall.

Pausing to take stock of his work, as do all experienced labourers who rest before they tire rather than when fatigue weakens their strength, Merlin looked upon the wall. It was still an ordinary stone wall, in every respect the same as it had been before he commenced his work. But for one difference. In the centre of the wall a door had appeared, made of dark oak boards under a low arch. Upon this door was carved the image of a dancing bear and the handle of the door was enmeshed in a looping, heavy blue chain that shimmered coldly in the shadows of the room.

Beyond this door the prophet could sense the presence of another time . . . He understood now that the curling mist had come from out of that time, and that within its clouds men were dead or dying, lost, broken, far from home. Violent sounds of screaming, shrill metal under stress, muffled roaring, tense shrieking of war engines unknown in his own time assailed Merlin's hearing as he stood facing north.

Here were decisions of some weight: how should these lost souls be passed from world to world; how would they find their way home; where, indeed, was their true home? Reaching within himself, Merlin took counsel as he had learned to do. For a moment nothing came and he seemed empty, poised over an abyss of silence, void of all being. Then a tight and potent verse arose complete within him. It came alive somewhere in his belly and rose up to fire his breast with inspiration; it pumped his lungs and burst forth into his throat, leaping from his lips even as tears sprang from his eyes; it set his head aflame with light and seethed into the outer air. The words that came were reflections, echoes, of its inner potency:

> I sit upon a high place
> On hard rock;
> I look upon a land,
> Ring of broken bells
> Song of flown bird,
> Anger of dead place,
> Murmur of lost people.
>
> No mere love may ease them
> No drug appease their pain,
> No sleep heal such wounds.
>
> Not I with my sight
> Or harp of hands,
> Not plucking strings
> Not singing back daylight,
> Nor I in the broken tree

The empty nut
Star clouded
On the drawing waiting height.

Nor you, a single child,
Nor any child of blood
Can open terror's eye,
Pluck forth the root
Then stem the deep born giant of the flood.

Up stone and under reach
In earth the warm veins leach
Out dark gold from waiting suns
Into web-ways for your gift.
Friends hand alone shall shape
The drowsy stone
Becoming joy to heal.

Distant is the time of which I speak,
Open is the heart on that wild day
To all pain, all voices of the weak,
All victims of the wheel.

Yet distant is come close
Upon this hilltop chair;
There is no moment of unwoven space
I may not touch,
No measure of unspiralled time
You may not share.

As Merlin uttered these words of power, he felt himself dissolve or reflect into countless images, mirrored within one another through an endless tunnel. When the first sound of the last word began, he felt the long-awaited response behind him in the south. Beyond his line of sight, behind his back, a great gate had opened into the worlds of light. Within that gate stood beings unknown to the human race, yet compassionate.

With the last letter of the last word, Merlin shattered the three bonds upon the door in the north: the shape, the colour, the sound. The blue chain melted like ice, the Bear symbol faded, the door become dull, unmoving wood. Then it split apart, exploding with the force of conflict in that place beyond. The dark opening filled with orange flames, flashing lights and ghastly momentary visions of a land utterly ruined.

Merlin gazed calmly upon the doorway until the first human shape appeared. It was a young man, rubbing his hand across his eyes as if he could not believe what he was seeing. He took a tentative step into the chamber, and Merlin saw his strange clothing of dull green and brown, his wooden and iron club held backwards, pointing before him, the narrow black handle outwards and the broad wooden striking blade tucked into his side. The young man's hair was grotesquely unnatural and short, his belts and straps were hung with small metal objects and amulets, their purpose obscure and sinister. One leg was ripped and bleeding, and for a moment the prophet almost reached out to take the wounded warrior in his arms and comfort him, but he knew that this one was the first of many. No mere comfort would suffice.

Within the shattered doorway they assembled, hardly daring at first to pass through, then slowly gathering momentum as if compelled by the many massing behind. Each seemed to re-form as he passed through, his shadow becoming substantial. Not one looked upon Merlin, as if the prophet was unseen or unreal to them.

As the terrible pressure of their passage increased, Merlin bowed his head and closed his eyes, anchoring himself within the memory of his own true time and place. He felt the unseen southern gate behind him drawing in the spirits of these strange warriors, and did not dare to turn and look upon their translation.

Like a rising gale they flowed past and over and through him, still clutching the redundant weapons of their world, still wearing their ugly garments. What they saw within the south Merlin could not assess. He knew that it was a vast, multifold realm of light, within which all elements were transmuted by that power known to him as the Dragons. He knew that it took many forms in many worlds, and that truth lay within and yet beyond them all.

The long night progressed, and with the dawn the last of the warriors had passed through the gate of the south. His shoulders slumped now and his body aching, Merlin looked upon the open door in the north. As he looked he became aware, with the last ebb of his exhausted perception, that some further terrible power lay just beyond that war-torn horizon, some mystery that he dared not fathom in his exhausted state. He thought of his own prophecies, uttered while still a child, and knew that the answer lay somewhere within them but was not for this night.

Behind his back he felt the bright resonance of the worlds of light expand momentarily to touch him, then snap shut. Deep within his mind he felt the words 'I am a Light and a Keeper of Lights . . .', the closing line of the ritual of the Doorkeeper uttered by the higher being that over-shadowed him. The northern wall blurred and resolved itself into simple stone at last. Merlin closed the circle with the four signs of peace, and gently washed his trembling hands in the bowl of mineral-red water. As the song of birds reached into the tower chamber, he stretched out upon his simple bed and slept.

R. J. Stewart

Here ends the Third Part, That of Return to the Source –
Wisdom Through Inspiration – The Light Within

AFTERWORD

◆

BARDS IN THE FUTURE

R. J. Stewart

e are moving into an age of instant media communication and this is often confused with instant wisdom. Knowledge changes from century to century, and although we can now move our information around more rapidly, it does not make us wiser. Wisdom comes through the fusing together of knowledge and actual experience, so there can never be virtual bards or cyber-druids.

The late anti-bard and prophet Andy Warhol predicted that in the future everyone would be famous for a few minutes, and of course he was correct. Rapid mass media brings rapid fame, rapid infamy, rapid oblivion. But the wisdom of the druid or druidess, the bard, the poet or poetess, is derived from long, slow absorption of the many interlinked traditions handed down from ancestral times. Without these we are simply product, with a fast-approaching sell-by date.

After absorbing tradition, we must find how to communicate its deepest lore, not merely through word-play or duplication but through regeneration. There is a subtle effect on consciousness from learning the older traditions, for they change us slowly and mysteriously. So being able to call up the complete Celtic/druidic information service on the Internet will do nothing for us unless we can then download it into our souls – not possible in this world.

So if we wish to go bard to the future, we must be ancestors to future wisdom, and create within ourselves the fertile ground of magical transformation. The material in this book gives some clues as to direction, but the quest has to be your own. The druid and bardic traditions have within them the keys that will open out our deepest source of inspiration, the source of being that is at the heart of all creation.

Appendix One

◆

Magical Story-telling

R. J. Stewart

The Origins and Traditions of Magical Tales

ne of the most enduring and important magical traditions is that of story-telling, yet it is the least represented in the twentieth-century revival of occult or esoteric arts and disciplines, possibly because it is the least understood. Magical story-telling derives from extremely ancient, primal spiritual arts, which originally expressed human understanding of the creation of the worlds. More simply, we might say that magical tales are a collective human echo of the story of all being; certain sacred story cycles and epics deriving from this primal story were active in Western culture until very recently, while in the East and in many remote areas of the planet such traditions still flourish.

Due to a vast flood of fantasy entertainment in both books and media, modern materialist cultures increasingly regard story-telling as 'mere fiction'; even the most remote human societies now have access to radio and television, and literacy or its lack is no longer relevant as a factor in cultural transformation. Thus what was once a magical and sacred matter of tradition is now easily supplanted and trivialized. It is worth emphasizing that this trivialization is as negative and effective for the sophisticated individual in a highly material or mechanized society as it is for the primal or isolated tribe.

The weaving of tales was of major importance to our ancestors, not merely for education or preservation of information, important as these were, but also for deep magical transformation. It is upon this level that we may reappraise the story-telling traditions for modern inner development, for this branch of magical art is long overdue for an empowered revival.

We do not have to retreat into a cosy, romantic pseudo-past, or even into a real but distant historical past, to find magical story-telling traditions. Such traditions are still active in relatively isolated areas of Europe, and are maintained by the native peoples of America and Australasia. In Western societies we find that there are well-documented examples of magical story cycles and heroic epics from Celtic culture – not only in medieval literature (though this preserved many important tales) but also in the twentieth century. Modern traditions of extended story-telling and mythical narratives are well known from several European countries, such as Scotland, Ireland, Finland and some other Scandinavian and Mediterranean regions. As such Western examples are directly relevant to our theme, we shall use them as our main source of initial discussion, before moving deeper into the magical creative process itself, but it should be kept in mind that they have many active, unbroken, traditional Eastern parallels which are not touched upon.

Before proceeding we must emphasize that *traditional* magical stories and story or epic cycles are not connected in any way with modern fantasy or 'magical' fiction; even when a writer has consciously borrowed motifs and symbols from genuine traditions, this does not guarantee that the resulting work will inevitably tap into magical or transformative levels of the original tradition.

Magical Tales Defined

What, then, is a magical tale? How does it differ from any inspired or contrived fantasy story? To this difficult but not impossible question we might add, what role, if any, can magical story-telling play in modern materialist culture, as it did in the past and as it still does in remote regions and societies? The first question can be answered in fairly precise terms, but the second can be truly answered only through experience, no matter what theory, methods of practice or examples may be offered upon a printed page or in an exploratory book of this sort.

Magical tales originally emerged from, and were preserved within, oral traditions. This does not imply that such tales were never written down, for a large number of them were recorded, often as they were passing out of widespread circulation. Arthurian literature of the Middle Ages is a typical example of such a recording and expansion of oral tradition, though we may easily lose sight of the original matter in its complex literary developments. The mythical and heroic sagas of Ireland are another example, and these were still being told in communal situations many centuries after monastic chroniclers first set them down in writing. It seems likely, with Irish and Scottish oral traditions, that the tales were mainly preserved intact through memory alone; in other words, they were not drawn from any of the now well-known and translated monastic sources, for these lay untranslated and forgotten until as late as the nineteenth century.

Wales produced a remarkable story cycle, much of which seems to have been lost, known as the *Mabinogion*, a term which, as we have seen, broadly means 'youthful adventures'. This magical and spiritual theme of youthful adventures is vitally important worldwide.

Thus we may define a magical story as being embedded within a tradition. This is an important rule, if accepted, for it immediately disposes of the bulk of modern fiction and fantasy, including many works claiming to be magical. Curiously, though, it does not dispose of all such matter and can include many odd items, such as certain vastly popular comic books that seem to preserve, albeit unconsciously, some of the old story-telling traditions.

Enduring magical tales, those that were part of long, organic, collective traditions of story-telling and preservation, were carefully formalized and stylized exercises of the imagination. They were assembled within strict yet flexible boundaries and held material for men, women and children of all ages. Certain cycles or types of tale seem to have had special group functions, as we know from comparative anthropology, but this aspect of story-telling is not directly relevant to our main theme, which is one of imagination and awareness rather than social development or custom. Furthermore, many of the reductionist conclusions of anthropology and psychology in connection with traditional lore worldwide may be open to criticism, and what seem to be sexual or peer-group roles, dramas, stories and the like to a city-based and psychologically trained university student may form part of much wider organic magical and spiritual traditions; the forest is thus ignored while categorizing individual clumps of trees.

Magical Tales, Visualization and Therapy

One hallmark of magical tales is that they involve familiar characters, often in varied guises, stylized and ritualized adventures, and a repetition that never palled upon the listener. We should always remember that they were recited aloud, with a teller performing to an assembled group. This is of key importance in the magical transformative function of story-telling, and has direct relevance to magical or spiritual disciplines, which frequently employ set groups of symbols and images in varied combinations, such as the tree of life, the tarot, the communion of saints and so forth. The familiarity and repetition of such units are not, paradoxically, boring and trivial, but lead to deep changes of consciousness in which the units or images, characters or symbols, reveal increasingly powerful harmonics of meaning and energy. We shall return to this important subject again.

In the modern arts of visualization or meditation and magical disciplines, guided imagery (sometimes incorrectly labelled 'pathworking') plays a significant role. Such esoteric visualization, in which the vital energies of the individual or group are directed through specific images and sequences, has been undertaken for thousands of years by priests, priestesses and magicians; it is part of a series of well-defined and long-established artistic disciplines, held in common by formal religions and magical traditions worldwide, each tradition expressing the art through its regional or national forms. Visualization has recently been 'discovered' as a therapeutic exercise by psychology, and this use of guided imagery, and indeed of freely generated story-telling, tends to mislead us into assuming that ancient traditions were similar in some way to our modern use. This is not the case.

The two extremes defined, that of inner discipline in visualization and creative imagery, and that of interactive but reductive mental therapy, are opposite or complementary poles in our intentional application of the potent forces of human imagination. Both draw upon an innate property of consciousness, that innermost creative act, a power which remains a mystery no matter what traditional or materialist claims are made to explain it.

Unique Aspects of the Story-telling Tradition

Magical story-telling is closer to the disciplines of the great magical or religious traditions than it is to any psychotherapeutic exercise, yet it does not partake fully of either function, while fulfilling the purposes of both. It has several levels of potential action: it may be therapeutic or simply educational and reassuring to the listeners, while being highly empowered for the teller. Those who wish to work with traditional imagery may, as has been repeatedly shown in modern interpretations, find that it holds many keys to deeper consciousness. This concept of keys to deeper or more potent levels of consciousness demands further consideration, as it is slightly different in the context of magical story-telling from that of direct meditation, prayer or ritual magic.

We can approach the inherent power of magical tales from a historical or cultural viewpoint, but it must be emphasized that this is valuable only as a foundation, and not as a statistical or purely historical or academic thesis. In traditional story-telling, which is the basis for any modern re-development of magical tales, the teller frequently recounts material from ancient cultural levels or sources. These may have been preserved for many centuries through theme, motif, character, imagery, actual archaic language, poetry and phrases. A mixture of contemporary material with older strata in a story-teller's traditional repertoire does not in any way detract from the astonishing preservation of ancient lore and language; indeed, it emphasizes the inherent sacred quality of such lore, that it remains honoured and enduring while contemporary matters come and go with each generation.

The Power of Language

In Ireland or the Western Isles of Scotland, we can find examples of twentieth-century story-tellers who recited long sagas from the heroic pagan Celtic era, handed down by word of mouth for many generations. Such story cycles eventually vanish when an old native language, in this case Gaelic, is supplanted by that of a dominant culture. Indeed, there is an important connection between language and magical story-telling: the subtle implications and harmonic connectives of traditional magical tales often do not survive translation, and certainly do not survive extensive changes of language within a community. 'The Creation of the World', which is the foundation of all magical tales, and 'The History of the Land and Its Inhabitants', which is the development and poetic unification of such tales, may be fully expressed only in the original languages of the people who generated and preserved their specific versions of the tales.

We find this vital concept corrupted in the popular and wildly inaccurate use of Hebrew in occult literature, even though the great majority of occult writers were not Hebrew speakers or of Jewish origin. In literature dealing with magical techniques, the key concept of a sacred language, known to all peoples in all places, had from the late seventeenth century onwards become confused through religious orthodoxy and conditioning, a confusion which resulted in lamentable ignorance of organic or native esoteric magical and spiritual traditions. This confusion is particularly apparent in the esoteric or magical texts of European writers in the nineteenth and early twentieth centuries, where misconceived and ill-understood Hebrew was freely mixed with Egyptian (then extremely fashionable), English, French and occasionally other languages.

Even in the late twentieth century, there is still a bizarre tendency to assume – incorrectly – that the West has no spiritual traditions other than orthodox Christianity, and that all deep insights must be imported from other cultures.

This whole sorry situation leads us to the conclusion that if we are to use language and story-telling in an empowered manner today, we must be certain that we employ languages which are a true part of our innermost lives. Thus there is a strong spiritual magical and psychological case for the use of English for English-speaking peoples, rather than a fantastical flight into superficially assimilated Hebrew, Sanskrit, Tibetan or other languages, so often used as a type of trivially élitist technical vocabulary of symbolism, spiritual dialectic or mystique, rather than mysticism.

In brief, our native tongue has the most potency and potential, whatever it may be. Material translated from different languages, however, may hold powerful images, concepts and insights; such potencies are, of course, universal rather than linguistic, national or racial. As has been touched upon above, subtle nuances from specific traditions can, unfortunately, be lost in translation; this is quite a different matter to loss of cultural cross-references or simple misunderstanding, and relates to the deep roots of language within consciousness.

The Deeper Levels of Magical Story-telling

Oral traditions, reaching deep into the roots of a tribal or national past and the collective relationship with the land are well attested by scholars worldwide, and are not in any sense rare or freakish. All people preserved, at one time, such a pool of ancestral poetry, imagery, lore, history and knowledge. Indeed, in non-literate cultures, living closely in touch with the environment, such tales were the sum of identity, wisdom and insight for the collective national tribal or family group. In certain individual cases, those of the dedicated magician, wise man or woman, or seer, such traditions were empowered to an even deeper level through special disciplines; but it is most significant that these initiatory arts employed the very same symbols as traditional tales and poems. In other words, the keys to inner power were found to be the common property of all, and not by any means a reserved or exclusive secret.

We find this concept again in the mystery religions of the ancient world, wherein well-known myths or tales were redefined and made the subjects of ritual drama and initiation. Despite the specialization and revelation, the foundational material was part of common consciousness – a legend, a hero, a group of gods and goddesses. Membership of a mystery revealed esoteric or deeper levels of a myth or religion, and worked towards profound transformations using the symbols of such myths in an empowered manner.

It is important to realize that traditional tales arise simultaneously from both early levels of culture and deep levels of consciousness. In superficial terms, it appears that the further back we travel in time (in a story), the further we are delving into ancestral imagination and awareness. This is a very different picture from the factual viewpoint of history, yet ancient tales preserve in a dream-like form many matters that have been verified in terms of academic history or archaeology.

Sacred Tales, Bardic Tradition and Tarot

In Eastern cultures today, it is said that blessings are earned by reciting and listening to certain sacred epics. The same benedictive quality was consciously ascribed to certain early Irish tales, and is clearly described and asserted in monastic texts, in which pagan tales were preserved, by orthodox Catholic monks and scribes, through their inherent traditional sanctity. Such long tales are always concerned with the creation of the world or worlds, and the adventures of the inhabitants, who range from gods to heroes, humans and animals.

A very similar pattern is found in the twelfth-century *Vita Merlini*, which preserves a complex creation and adventure cycle woven around Merlin, drawn in part from Welsh or Breton bardic traditions by Geoffrey of Monmouth. The tarot, which seems to have first appeared in the form of illustrated cards in Italy during the Renaissance, is very likely drawn from such a story-telling or bardic cycle of images dealing with creation and transformative adventures. Such blessed tales were originally found in all lands, but have now virtually died away in Western civilization. So, if we are to reinstate magical tale-telling or tale-generation, it must fulfil certain basic requirements: first, it must employ a living language and not be stuffed with false or exotic vocabulary, and, second, it must fulfil the magical role of virtually lost oral traditions in a manner suitable for modern culture.

Interestingly, tarot fulfilled certain aspects of that role when it first appeared as formal picture cards, which were used for story-telling in southern Europe for several centuries. Today there is a considerable revival of tarot, much of which is trivial, dull or absurd; in this revival, story-telling is once again being linked to tarot. If a traditional cycle of symbols, situations and characters from mythic tale-telling was the source of tarot, as seems very likely, then, that tarot provides one significant route back into that primal creative mode of consciousness.

But we must be very wary indeed of using tarot for rule-of-thumb trivial exercises in assembling meaningless 'symbolic' narratives, just as we must take care not to prostitute the enormous potential of tarot into crude, immature fortune-telling. In this context of tarot and European story-telling traditions, we might emphasize that the old tellers did not merely draw cards and talk through or improvise from the images that appeared. Each card or combination acted as a trigger, or sometimes as mnemonic, for portions of a vast oral repertoire already firmly established within the story-teller's memory and imagination. Perhaps the best-known parallel might be the ancient Greek epics of the *Iliad* and the *Odyssey*, ascribed to Homer, in which many separate tales, motifs and images were assembled from traditional myth and legend by a master poet.

Magical Tales and Collective Consciousness

Although traditional tales were preserved by individual and highly respected tellers, they originated in what might be called a transpersonal realm or mode of awareness. This cannot be over-emphasized: there were no 'authors' of traditional magical tales, which were organic and anonymous. We might be strongly tempted to say that they were the products of the 'unconscious', as defined by Jungian psychology and other modern schools of the psyche, but although this definition is adequate and proper in its modern therapeutic context, it does not encompass or even approach the traditional magical tales and epic cycles of non-literate cultures. There are profound distances and differences between the use of improvisation in therapy and the anonymous cosmological, magical and initiatory tales preserved collectively worldwide.

The key to magical story-telling, with its undeniably therapeutic and transformative powers, is more likely to be found within esoteric psychology, those studies of human consciousness made and taught for millennia before our modernist revival and development of psychotherapy. Indeed, we can be more precise and assert that one of the main keys to the power of magical tales lies in the *visualizing* of emblems or personae within them. Other essential factors must also be present, but we can consider the importance of visual units briefly at this stage.

As mentioned above, a major art in esoteric or inner development, regardless of school or religion, is creative visualization. It may be firmly limited and guided, as in Jesuit disciplines or in certain Eastern religions, or it may employ a certain degree of free association set within a defined tradition. Such defined traditions are those of symbolic or imaginal 'alphabets', which are sets of gods and goddesses, other characters, attributes within a cosmology and so forth. Esoteric arts and sciences use well-known sets, such as the tree of life, the three worlds, the wheel of life or the tarot to great effect.

Bard, Poets and the Power and Art of Memory

A process similar to the magical 'alphabets' but less defined and controlled was used by the old traditional story-tellers. This may be one of the reasons for their prodigious, almost unbelievable, memories, for they often had enormous repertoires and could recite tales that lasted for hours or even days, and remember perfectly a story that had been heard only once, and retell it accurately many years later. Such feats of memory are well attested by scholars, collectors and researchers into tradition. But are they feats of memory in the modern sense, where one has to accumulate data in an order and then work to replicate that order in verbal and conscious patterns? Undoubtedly they are of a different nature.

An example might help us to consider this link between visualization and memory, and how it applies to the transformative power inherent within magical story-telling. A tape-recording made by the School of Scottish Studies, interviewing an old Gaelic story-teller, clearly defines his method of memory. He says (in Gaelic) that he remembers the tales because he sees them as pictures upon the wall – in other words, as a projected and connected series of images. The images enabled him to regenerate the words associated with each image. Furthermore, he had learned the tales by listening to a story-teller when he was young and attuning to the images, the pictures upon the wall. When he knew the pictures, the words came automatically, as if they could not be separated from one another.

It is interesting to note that the Gaelic story-teller projected the images 'upon the wall', as this is precisely one of the ancient techniques taught within magical and meditative schools, where the use of walls, mirrors or the magical implements, the disc or shield, are all employed to give a field for the imaginative energies to become defined and active. We must remember that such examples from folk tradition are organic or innocent; there is no question of the tellers being part of a so-called 'occult' movement. In some localities, however, it would be reasonable to suggest they were the last remnants of an old bardic caste, particularly as tale-telling and ballad-singing ran in specific families for many generations. The bards, in turn, were originally an order within the pagan druid priesthood. In Ireland, Scotland and some northern European countries, this definition of a special role for the poet and reciter of traditional lore was preserved well into the nineteenth and early twentieth centuries.

An organic unity was noted from traditional ballad-singers in Britain and America by nineteenth- and early-twentieth-century folklore and folksong collectors; singers repeatedly asserted that the music and the long ballad stories were inseparable, and that to know one was to know the other. The same is frequently found in the learning of traditional dances: to know the music is to know the dance steps. This is clearly 'remembering' of a very different type from that usually employed in education; and the unification or harmonic merging of images, music, dance steps and so forth is far too widespread and well attested to be passed off as a mere matter of poor education or lack of explanatory ability on the part of ignorant participants.

The visual aspects of oral tradition, which link closely to magical imagery, with so many characters drawn from ancient religion and deep ancestral themes, have hardly been studied at all. There are many resonances of the classical art of memory, formalized by the ancients and preserved in a number of medieval scholastic texts. A detailed analysis of this art is found in Frances Yates's book *The Art of Memory*, and there is certainly some connection between traditions of immense memory in story-telling and a lost classical art which may have originally come out of the temples of the pagan world. The remnants of this system seem to have been directed towards oratory, but it has many implications of a more profound origin.

But we are not talking of a conscious orator's skill: rather we are dealing with an organic tradition rooted in primal magic. The images are not merely present as aids to memory but are empowered magical images of gods, goddesses, heroes, adventures, other worlds and dimensions, and mysterious creatures. It is upon this level that magical story-telling may be reinstated for modern expansion of consciousness.

Modern Magical Tales

How, therefore, do we define or create and employ a magical tale for modern use? There is, of course, considerable danger in attaching intellectual or systematic interpretations to stories, be they psychological, materialist or esoteric. But despite this risk, there are certain specific functions or roles of the specifically magical tale which differ from those of stories in general fiction. As mentioned above, attuning to a tradition is perhaps the most important, and allowing that tradition to regenerate fruitfully and harmoniously within a modern style and literary or – far less common nowadays – spoken context. But there are other more specific requirements of a magical tale, which are often absent from modern fantasy, even when it claims an overtly 'magical' theme.

Perhaps the most curious and obscure example concerns attuning to other worlds and times. The hallmark is that we feel such worlds and times to be most real, not as a matter of suspension of disbelief but in an intuitive and sometimes painful flow of recognition. In other words, certain magical tales are not symbolic, allegorical, poetic or spiritually enlivened in the sense of wisdom tales or potent visualizations; they are instead, windows, into real places, real times, real people. The magic is inherent not only in the connection between our imagination and those other worlds or times, but in the interplay between our consciousness and those places and people. This phenomenon is well known in esoteric spiritual or magical arts, though it is seldom discussed adequately, and may give rise to absurd claims and wild nonsense on the part of those who would like to be known for contacting other worlds and so fantasize something exotic or grandiose to inflate their self-esteem.

Images, Visualization and Ritual

Magical tales were, originally, a collective route, a path towards inner transformation. They provided the reassurance, entertainment and education of well-established cultural traditions, but could, if required, be taken several steps further. Like the ancient mysteries, they had an exoteric or outer meaning and function, and an esoteric or inner one. The paradox of true spiritual tradition, embodied in collective or oral traditions world-wide, is that the esoteric function is totally explicit in the outer form; there are no hidden schools of obscure interpretations or deep hidden secrets. Anyone making grandiose contact claims is unlikely to have attuned to a genuine tradition.

To create a magical tale for the modern reader or listener, the creator must tap into a genuine magical tradition, and not merely write about something quaint or 'magical'. To employ a modern magical tale, the reader or listener must build the images in his or her imagination. This is far more important than any intellectual assessment, though there are frequently and properly intellectual levels and substance to the symbolism and patterns in magical tales.

But esoteric literature abounds in recondite, obscure, intellectual expositions, interpretations, methods, techniques and theories. The magical tale, however, like the magical ballad or song, should act directly upon the consciousness through its imagery, while the intellectual content operates not only through the logical processes but transcends them by acting from a higher level of consciousness altogether. So it is possible to give keys to or interpretations of magical tales, but the keys are not in any way essential to the magic or transformative force of the imagery, pattern and characters or events within the tale itself. Indeed, excessive interpretation can lessen the impact of magical tales; they are generated from and should speak directly to the deepest areas of the imagination, regardless of interpretation.

There is a well-known and easily detected odour of falseness to things contrived by assembling 'symbolism'. Popular psychology has much to answer for in this respect, as is demonstrated extensively in many forms of commercial advertising, in some 'psychologized' schools of novel-writing or drama and screenplay, and in certain of the visual arts. Thus it is easy and eminently possible to assemble a good set of magical symbols into a plausible narrative; but this does not necessarily make a magical tale.

Like the creation of artificial life-forms in popular fiction, the meaningful union of proper, even healthy, parts does not make a living entity. The result is often a rotten corpse or a potentially dangerous monster; once again, advertising or perhaps pop-music videos give many examples of such potential pollution or enervation of the imagination.

One highly effective method of working with traditional magical tales and ballads which may sometimes be applied to modern magical tales is to take to structural phases of the narrative and the visual images as sources for ritual pattern-making. This is merely a more sophisticated version of the centuries-old tradition of dancing or acting out narrative tales and ballads. It consists of applying the elements of the tale within the master glyphs of magic, such as the fourfold circle, or the tree of life, and generating a dramatic or ceremonial sequence from them.

It should be emphasized most strongly that this technique is not the same as psychodrama or ritual enactment used in psychotherapy, and that it can lead to very powerful forces and deeply transformative experiences. Whereas role play in psychotherapy or counselling may be, in some cases, beneficial, magical ritual taps into vast imaginative traditions enduring through many centuries, and has a number of very potent and well-established effects. Most important of all, magical ritual or ceremonial drama is not, and never has been, intended as 'therapy'. It forms one of the ancient techniques of willed inner transformation and redirection of vital energies, and usually demands that the operator or celebrant be as psychically mature and well balanced as possible. Having said all of this there are obviously many stages of development and levels of technique and ability between the two extremes of trivial therapeutic role play and empowered ritual. Magical tales are one method of enlivening the psyche yet avoiding some of the pitfalls inherent in either materialist psychology or esoteric arts.

APPENDIX TWO

◆

THE DESIGN OF THE CIRCULAR TEMPLES AND CROMLECHS OF THE DRUIDS

Original Documents Relative to the Celebrated Structure of Stonehenge*

he superstition of the Britons, as we find it delineated in the ancient Bards, and probably, as it existed for many centuries, before the time of any of those Bards which are now extant, appears to have been a heterogeneous system, in which the memorials of the patriarch, and of the deluge, and some of the true principles of the patriarchal religion, were blended with a mass of absurdity, and an idolatrous worship of the host of heaven.

Thus, whilst *Ceridwen* is the genius of the Ark, we observe, that at the same time, the *moon* is her representative in the heavens. Her husband, *Tegid* or *Saidi*, commemorates *Noah*; but he is also viewed in the planet *Saturn*; and by the name of *Hu*, he even takes possession of the solar orb. *Avagddu*, the *black accumulation*, which appalled the world at the deluge, has brightened into *Rhuvawn Bevyr*, or the *splendor or the regenerated sun*.

Hence we must expect to find, that the temples which were sacred to this motley superstition, had some reference to the *celestial*, as well as to the *terrestrial* objects of adoration.

It has been already remarked, that *Cadeiriath Saidi*, or *the language of the chair of Saidi*, was personified; and that he constituted an important character in British mythology.

But such an ideal personage as this, could have been nothing more than a representative of the sacred *ceremonies*, *doctrine*, *laws*, and *institutes* of Druidism: as exhibited and taught, in the temple or sanctuary of Ceridwen, and, of the other mythological group.

This temple was named *Caer Sidi*, the *circle, or sanctuary of Sidi*; and Taliesin's presidency, as high priest in that temple, was styled *Cadair Caer Sidi*, the *chair of Caer Sidi*. The doctrine and the law which he pronounced from that *chair*, were therefore, the *Cadeiriath*, or *language of the chair*. Let us now inquire, why the name of *Caer Sidi* was appropriated to the Druidical temples.

I might cut this matter short, by asserting upon the authority of Mr Bryant, that *Sidi*, or Σιδη, was one of the names of Ceres.

*Extract from The Mythology and Rites of the British Druids, Edward Davies, 1809

As the Ark, says that great mythologist, was looked upon as the mother of mankind, and stiled *Da-Mater*, so it was figured under the resemblance of the Ροια, *Pomegranate*, since abounding with seeds, it was thought no improper emblem of the Ark, which contained the rudiments of the future world. Hence the deity of the Ark was named *Rhoia*, and was the *Rhea* of the Greeks. – Another name of the pomegranate was *Sidè* (Σιδη, *Sidec*) of which name there was a city in *Pamphylia*, and another in Boeotia, which was said to have been built by SIDE the daughter of Danaus, which may be in a great measure true: for *by a daughter of Danaus*, is meant 'a priestess of *Da-Naus*, the Ark,' the same as Da-Mater.

According to this deduction, *Sidee* must have been as legitimate a name as *Rhea*, for the genius of the Ark; and it must have represented that sacred vessel, as hitherto *impregnated with its seeds*; or, as containing the patriarch and his family, who became objects of superstitious veneration, to succeeding ages.

But the British Caer *Sidi* was derived through another channel. It appears from the *spoils of the deep*, one of the principal of the mys-tical poems of Taliesin, that the original Caer Sidi, and the prototype of that sanctuary, in which our Bard presided was no other than the *sacred vessel*, in which the mythological *Arthur* and *his seven friends escaped the general deluge*. Thus the Britons regarded *Caer Sidi* as a name of the *Ark*.

But as the Britons, like many other heathens, had blended their commemorations of the patriarch and his family, with the worship of the host of heaven; as the *sun, moon,* and *planets*, were now viewed as emblems of their consecrated progenitors, and of their sacred ship, and probably had engrossed the greatest part of popular veneration; so we find that the name of *Caer Sidi*, or *Sidin*, was transferred from the sacred ship, to that *great circle*, in which those luminous emblems of their gods presided and expatiated. In British astronomy, it was become the name of the *Zodiac*.

Agreeably to the idiom of the Welsh language, the words *Caer Sidi*, or *Sidin*, imply the *circle*, or *inclosed place* of the *revolution*. We may, therefore, admire the dexterity with which the genius of mythology appropriated the title, first, to the *vessel* in which *all the surviving inhabitants of the world performed the greatest revolution* recorded in history; secondly, to *that celestial circle*, in which the luminaries of the world *perpetually revolve*; and lastly, to the *Druidical temples*, which appear from the works of the Bards, to have had a marked reference, both to the *sacred ship*, and to the *Zodiac*.

Their reference to the former may be proved, not only from the *spoils of the deep*, but also from Taliesin's poem upon the sons of *Llŷr*, where he tells us, that his chair, or presidency, was sacred to Ceridwen.

Neud amug ynghadeir o beir Ceridwen!
Handid rydd fy nhafawd,
Yn addawd gwawd Ogyrwen.

Is not my chair protected by the cauldron of Ceridwen?
Therefore, let my tongue be free
In the sanctuary of the praise of the goddess.

And again, in the same poem, he names and describes this presidency:

Ys cyweir fy nghadeir yng**haer** Sidi
Nis plawdd haint a henaint a fo yndi
Ys gwyr Manawyd a Phryderi
Tair Orian y am dan a gan rhegddi
Acam ei bannau ffrydieu gweilgi
A'rffynawn ffrwythlawn yssydd odduchti
Ys whegach nor' gwîn gwyn y llyn yndi.

Complete is my chair in *Caer Sidi*
Neither disorder nor age will oppress him that is within it.
It is known to *Manawyd* and *Pryderi*,
That three loud strains round the fire, will be sung before it;
Whilst *the currents of the sea are round its borders,*
And *the copious fountain is open from above,*
The liquor within it is sweeter than delicious wine.

It is clear, from these remarkable passages, that the name of *Caer Sidi* was given to the sanctuary, in which the rites of Ceridwen were celebrated: for the presidency which was protected by the *cauldron of Ceridwen,* and the presidency of *Caer Sidi,* imply one and the same thing. And the sanctuary of that presidency is described with circumstances, which can be referred only to the history of a ship, and which evidently allude to the Ark.

The *currents of the deep compass it about,* and the *copious fountain is open from above;* still there is safety, tranquillity, and comfortable subsistence within. All this is the literal history of the Ark, and there can be little doubt, but that it is also the history of some rites, which the Britons observed in commemoration of it.

That the same sanctuary had its allusion to the great circle of the Zodiac, may be inferred from the language of the same Taliesin, who vaunting of the high importance of his pontifical office, assimilates his own character with that of *Apollo,* or the sun.

Having informed us, in the poem which is called *his history,* that he had received the *Awen,* or *inspiration,* from the cauldron of *Ceridwen,* he concludes in this manner.

Mi a fum ynghadair flin
Uwch Caer Sidin
A honno ya troi fydd
Rhwng tri elfydd
Pand rhyfedd ir byd
Nas argennyd.

I have presided in a toilsome *chair,*
Over the *circle of Sidin,*
Whilst that is continuously revolving between three elements;
Is it not a wonder to the world,
That men are not *enlightened?*

Here the Bard, as usual, blends the description of *celestial* objects with that of their *representatives* on earth. The *Caer Sidin,* which continually revolves in the midst of the universe, is the *circle of the zodiac.* Here the *sun,* the great luminary of the world, is the *visible president.* Our Bard could not pretend to have presided in *this Caer Sidin*; but as his own assumed name, *Taliesin, radiant front*, was a mere title of the sun, so, as chief Druid of his age, he was the priest and *representative* of the *great luminary* upon earth; and his vice-regent in that sanctuary, which typified *the abode of the gods*.

In the subject of British antiquities, it might be deemed of some importance to ascertain the form of those *Caer Sidis*, or sanctuaries, in which our ancestors celebrated the rites of their *Ceridwen* or *Ceres*, and performed other acts or worship – to determine whether those sanctuaries consisted merely of *caves, glades* in the sacred *groves, islets* in the *lakes* or margin of the sea, and the like; or whether they are to be recognized in those *round trenches* and *circles of stones*, which still remain in various parts of these islands, and have been deemed Druidical temples. I shall therefore offer such hints upon the subject as occur to me, and leave them to the consideration of mythologists and antiquaries.

As the Britons distinguished the *zodiac* and the *temples*, or sanctuaries of their gods, by the same name of *Caer Sidi*, and as their great Bard, Taliesin, blends the *heavenly* and the *terrestrial Sidi* in one description, we may presume, that they regarded the *latter* as a type of representation of the *former*.

The two great objects of their superstitious regard, as we have already seen, were the *patriarch* and the *ark*; but under the names of *Hu* and *Ceridwen*, these were figured or represented by the two great *luminaries*, which revolve in the celestial zone. And this conceit was analogous to the mythology of other nations. For *Liber Pater* was the same as *Dionusus*, who, according to Mr Bryant, was the patriarch Noah; and *Ceres* was the genius of the ark: yet we find that Virgil, the most learned of the poets, unites their characters with those of the *sun* and *moon*.

> – *Vos, O clarissima mundi*
> *Lumina, labantem calo qui ducitis annum*
> *Liber, et alma Ceres!*

> O Liber, and holy Ceres,
> ye bright luminarics of the world,
> who lead forth the year, revolving in the heavens!

Were a representation of this idea of the poet, to be made in sculpture, we should see two great mythological characters moving in their proper *orbits*, amongst the *signs* of the *zodiac*, which mark the different seasons of the *revolving year*, and which the Egyptians style *the grand assembly*, or *senate of the twelve gods*.

In Mons, de Gebelin's Monde Primitif, I observe a curious antique design, taken from the zone of a statue, supposed to be that of Venus, which is highly illustrative of this subject. Here, the story of Ceres and Proserpine is beautifully told. The former goddess is mounted upon a car, formed like a *boat* or *half moon*, and drawn by *dragons*; holding lighted torches in her hands, she flies in search of her daughter, who is violently carried away in Pluto's chariot. Hercules, or the *sun*, leads the procession, and the group is hastening into the presence of Jupiter, who appears enthroned on a cloud. The whole is surrounded with *twelve oblong tablets*, or *short pillars*, upon which are depicted the twelve signs of the zodiac, in an erect posture; intimating evidently, that the mythology of those personages was connected with an exact observation of the stars, and of the return of the seasons. And, agreeably to this hint, we find that the mystical Bards, and tales of the Britons, constantly allude to the completion of the *year*, and the return of a particular *day*, when they treat of the history and the rites of Ceridwen.

Were a *pantheon*, or *temple of the assembled gods*, to be designed *after the model of this sculpture*, we should have the principal figures stationed in the central area, and the *pillars* of the constellations ranged about them in a *circle*. And were this to be undertaken, by a people who abhorred *covered temples*, and either *disallowed the use of sculpture*, or else *were ignorant of the art*; the central figures would be represented by *rude masses* of wood or stone, and the *rude* pillars of the constellations would occupy the outward circle, as in the *British monuments, delineated by Dr Borlase and other antiquaries*.

That the Druidical temples were generally of a round form, appears by the appellative terms which the Bards constantly use in describing them, as *Caer Sidi*, the *circle* of *revolution*; *Côr*, a *round or circle*, *Cylch*, a *circle*; and *Cylch Byd*, the *circle of the world*, which occurs in *Aneurin* and *Taliesin*.

It is also evident, that they were composed of *stone*: for *Aneurin, Taliesin*, and *Merddin*, speak of the *stones* which composed these circles. But let us endeavour to identify *one* of their circular temples, that we may have some rule to judge the rest.

In the poems of Hywel, the son of Owen, that prince says expressly, that *the proud-wrought inclosure in the Gyvylchi, in the desert of Arvon, in Eryri, or Snowden, and towards the shore*, was the *Caer*, or *sanctuary of the mystical goddess*, and the *chosen place of her daughter Llywy*, or the *British Proserpine*.

The topography of this temple is so minutely pointed out, that the spot cannot be mistaken: and if we find here a monument which has any appearance of representing the Zodiac, or *Celestial Caer Sidi*, it may serve as a guide, in distinguishing other British monuments of the same kind.

Dwy-*Gyvylchi* is still known, as the name of a parish, in the very spot where the Cambrian prince fixes his *Caer Wen Glaer*, or *sanctuary of the illustrious Lady*, in the *deserts of Arvon*, in *Eryri*, and *towards the sea*: and here the remains of the *Caer* are still to be found.

The annotator upon Camden [Gibson], having described a strong fortress, 'seated on the top of one of the highest mountains, of *that part of Snowden, which lies towards the sea*', gives the following account of this ancient temple:

> About a mile from this fortification, stands the most remarkable monument in all Snowden, called *Y Meineu Hirion*, upon the plain mountain, within the parish of Dwy-*Gyvycheu*, above Gwddw Glâs. It is a *circular entrenchment*; about twenty-six yards diameter; on the outside whereof, are certain *rude, stone pillars*; of which about *twelve* are now standing, some two yards, and others five foot high: and these are again encompassed with a stone wall. It stands upon the plain mountain, as soon as we come to the height, having much even ground about it; and not far from it, there are three other *large stones*, pitched on end, in a *triangular form*.

We are also told that, at the distance of about three furlongs from this monument, there are several huge heaps, or *Carns*, and also *cells*, constructed of huge stones, fixed in the ground, and each cell covered with one or two stones of a superior size.

Such was the sanctuary which was held sacred to *Ceridwen* and *Llywy*, or *Ceres* and *Proserpine*, in the middle of the *twelfth* century, an age in which the honours of those characters were not forgotten: for we have already seen, that their mysteries, strange as the fact may appear, were still celebrated, not only with toleration, but also under the patronage of the British princes.

Hywel's avowed veneration of those mysteries, into which he himself had been initiated, would not have permitted him to speak lightly, and at random, upon the subject of this hallowed fane. And his own studious disposition, joined with his rank in society, must have procured him access to the best information, respecting the antiquities of his country, had any deep research been requisite. But this case presented no difficulty. There could have been no doubt of the intention of a temple, which was sacred to an *existing superstition*. A regular succession of mystical Bards had hitherto been maintained, from the days of Taliesin, and from the ages of pure Druidism.

Hence, my comparing this structure with the facts previously stated, we may fairly conclude, that in those ages, the temples which were sacred to British mysteries, were regarded as images of *Caer Sidi*, or the Zodiac, as they were dignified with its name, or else were so constructed as to represent some of the *phænomena*, displayed in that celestial zone.

In this monument of the *Gyvylchi*, we find the *circle of twelve stones*, which undoubtedly represented the twelve signs, the same which appeared upon the Antique, published by M. De Gebelin, commemorative of the history of Ceres and Proserpine.

From the description quoted out of Camden, imperfect as it is, we may infer, that the temple of Gyvylchi is a work of the same kind as those circular monuments of stone, which have attracted the notice of the curious, from the South to the North extremity of this Island, and which our best antiquaries pronounce, not only to have been temples of the heathen Britons, but also to have been constructed upon *astronomical principles*: in short, to have represented, either the Zodiac itself, or certain *cycles* and *computations*, deduced from the study of astronomy. Hence the frequent repetition of *twelve*, *nineteen*, *thirty*, or *sixty* stones, which has been remarked in the circles of these monuments.

Our fane of Snowden, it is admitted, could never have vied in magnificence, with a *Stonehenge*, or an *Abury*. In the ages of Druidism, it could have been regarded only as a *provincial* sanctuary, but the number of *twelve* stones which constitutes its circle is *twice* repeated in the stupendous fabric of *Abury*; it frequently occurs also, in the Cornish monuments, noted by Dr Borlase; and it is found in the complete temple of *Classerniss*, in the Western Isles of Scotland. Here is also the *cell*, consisting of three huge stones, erected in a *triangular form*, as in the structure of Abury.

From this little Cambrian chapel, then let us endeavour to trace our way to the larger monuments of British superstition.

That *Stonehenge* was a Druidical temple of high eminence, and that its construction evinces considerable proficiency in astronomy, has been the decided opinion of many respectable antiquaries. That I may not multiply proofs of a fact so generally known, I shall only extract part of the learned Mr Maurice's remarks upon that celebrated monument.

But all of the circular temples of the Druids, (says the author of the Indian Antiquities) as Stonehenge is the most considerable, a

description of it from the most ancient and the most modern writer on that subject – is here presented to the reader. I take it for granted, that the passage cited by *Diodorus*, from *Hecatæus*, and before alluded to by Mr Knight, is [to be understood of] *this identical temple of Stonehenge*, or *Choir Gaur*, its ancient British name, meaning, according to Stukeley, the *Great Cathedral* or *Grand Choir*; and surely, no *national church* could ever better deserve that distinguished appellation.

The author then quotes the passage from Diodorus, respecting the *Hyperborean* temple of *Apollo*, to which he adds the following remark: 'Such is the account given near two thousand years ago, *of this circular temple*, FOR IT COULD MEAN NO OTHER, by Diodorus the Sicilian, from a writer still prior in time.'

Mr Maurice, in the next place, extracts the description which is given of the same monument, in Mr Gough's edition of Camden;and these are his remarks upon it:

There is no occasion for my troubling the reader with any extended observations, on these accounts of Stonehenge. Whoever has read, or may be inclined to read my history of oriental architecture, as connected with the astronomical, and mythological notions of the ancients, printed in the third volume of this work – may see most of the assertions realized, in the form and arrangement of *this old Druid temple*. For, in the first place, it is *circular*, as it is there proved, all ancient temples to the *Sun* and *Vesta* – were. In the second place, the *Adytum* or *Sanctum Sanctorum*, is of an *oval* form, representing the *Mundane egg*, after the manner that all those adyta, in which *the sacred fire perpetually blazed* – were constantly fabricated. In the third place, the situation is fixed astronomically, as we shall make fully evident when we come to speak of Abury: the grand entrances, both of this temple, and that superb monument of antiquity, being placed exactly North-east, as all the *gates* or portals of the ancient caverns, and cavern temples were; especially those dedicated to *Mithra*, that is, the sun.

In the fourth place, the number of stones and uprights (in the outward circle) making together, exactly *sixty*, plainly alludes to that peculiar, and prominent feature of *Asiatic* astronomy, the sexagenary cycle – while the number of stones, forming the minor circle of the cove, being exactly *nineteen*, displays to us the famous *Metonic*, or rather *Indian* cycle; and that of *thirty*, repeatedly occurring, the celebrated age, or generation of the Druids.

Fifthly, the temple being *uncovered*, proves it to have been erected under impressions, similar to those which animated the ancient Persians, who rejected the impious idea of confining the Deity – within – an inclosed shrine, however magnificent, and therefore, consequently, at all events, it must have been erected before the age of Zoroaster, who flourished more than five hundred years before Christ, and who first covered in the Persian temples.

And finally, the heads and horns of oxen and other animals, found on the spot prove that the sanguinary rites, peculiar to the *Solar superstition* – were actually practised, within the awful bounds of this hallowed circle.

I have omitted a few clauses, in which the ingenious author derives the *British*, immediately from the *Indian* superstition; partly because his opinion might appear to disadvantage, unsupported by the arguments which are adduced in various parts of this dissertation; and partly because I have some kind of evidence, that what was exotic in the system of the Britons, came to them by the way of *Cornwall*, and therefore was probably derived to them from the *Phœnicians*.

Our learned author's opinion of the dignity of this structure, of the knowledge of astronomy displayed in its plan, and its destination as a heathen temple, I should suppose will hardly be disputed. Yet still, those gentlemen who assert, that *the Druids left no monuments behind them*, but *their venerated oaks*, will pertinaciously contend, that *no evidence has been produced* to connect the design of this stupendous pile, with the national superstition of the Britons.

It appears to me, however, that *considerable evidence of this connection does exist*; and I hope, I shall not perform an unacceptable office to the public in bringing it forward.

BIBLIOGRAPHY

Boswell, J., The Journal of a Tour to the Hebrides with Dr Samuel Johnson, London, 1941

Bowen, D., *Ancient Siluria*, Llanerch Publishers, Felinfach, Wales, 1992

Branston, B., *The Lost Gods of England*, Thames & Hudson, London, 1974

Brennan, M., *The Stars and the Stones*, Thames & Hudson, London, 1983

Briard, J., *The Bronze Age in Barbarian Europe* Routledge & Kegan Paul, London, 1978

Bromwich, R., *Dafydd ap Gwilym*, Gower, 1992

Bryce, D., *Symbolism of the Celtic Cross*, Llanerch Publishers, Felinfach, Wales

Bryce, D., (ed.), *The Herbal Remedies of the Physicians of Myddfai*, Llanerch Publishers, Felinfach, Wales

Bryce, D. (trans.), *Celtic Folk Tales from Armorica*, Llanerch Publishers, Felinfach, Wales, 1985

– *The Celtic Legend of the Beyond*, Llanerch Publishers, Felinfach, Wales

Burl, A., *The Stone Circles of the British Isles*, Yale University Press, New Haven, 1976

Campbell, J. G., *Witchcraft and the Second Sight in the Highlands and Islands of Scotland*, Glasgow, 1902

Child, F. J., *The English and Scottish Popular Ballads*, Boston, 1892–8

Clarke, B. (trans.), *The Vita Merlini* (of Geoffrey of Monmouth), University of Wales, Cardiff, 1973

Cumont, F., *Oriental Religions in Roman Paganism*, Dover Books, New York, 1956

Ellis, Ossian, *The Story of the Harp in Wales*, University of Wales, Cardiff, 1980

Evans-Wentz, W. Y., *Fairy Faith in Celtic Countries*, Oxford, 1911

Gantz, J. (trans.), *The Mabinogion*, Penguin Books, Harmondsworth, 1976

Gardner, A., *A Book of Highland Verse*, Paisley, Scotland, 1910

Giles, J. A. (trans.), *The History of the Kings of Britain*, London, 1896

Jones, E., *Musical and Poetic Relics of the Welsh Bards*

Lang, A., *History of Scotland* (various editions), 3 vols.

Lang, L., *Orkney and Shetland*, David & Charles, Newton Abbot, 1974

– *Late Celtic Britain and Ireland*, Methuen, London, 1975

Levis, J. H., *The British King who Tried to Fly*, West Country Editions, Bath, 1919 (reprinted 1973)

MacCana, P., *Celtic Mythology*, Hamlyn, London, 1975

MacCulloch, J. A., *The Religion of the Ancient Celts*, Edinburgh, 1911

– *The Celtic and Scandinavian Religions*, Hutchinson, London, 1948

Macleod, F., 'Iona' in *The Works of Fiona Macleod*, Heinemann, London, 1927

Macmillan, A., *Iona*, Its *History, Antiquities, etc.*, London and Glasgow, 1898

Martin, M., *A Description of the Western Islands of Scotland*, 1703 (reprinted 1934)

Marwick, E. W., *The Folklore of Orkney and Shetland*, Batsford, London, 1975

Matheson, W. (ed.), *The Blind Harper: Songs of Roderick Morrison & His Music*, Scottish Gaelic Texts Society

Morgan, Morien O., *The Mabin of the Mabinogion* RILKO, London

Morgannwg, Iolo, *Barddas/Myrvyrian Archaiology/Manuscripts*, The Welsh Text Society, Wales

Murphy, G., *Ossianic Lore*, Mercier Press

Murray, J. A. H., *Thomas of Erceldoune*, Early English Text Society, London, 1875

Parry, J. J. (trans.), *The Vita Merlini* (of Geoffrey of Monmouth), University of Urbana, Illinois, 1925

Pennar, M. (trans.), *Taliesin Poems*, Llanerch Publishers, Felinfach, Wales

Piggot, S., *The Druids*, Penguin Books, Harmondsworth, 1974

Porter, H. M., *The Celtic Church in Somerset*, Morgan Books, Bath, 1971

Quiggin, E. C., *Prologomena to the Study of the Later Irish Bards 1200–1500*, America Committee for Irish Studies

Raine, K., *A Choice of Blake's Verse*, Faber & Faber, London

Ratcliffe Barnett, T., *Border By-Ways and Lothian Lore*, Edinburgh, 1937

Rees, A. and B., *Celtic Heritage*, Thames & Hudson, 1961

Roberts, E. Ernest, *With Harp, Folktale and Fiddle*

Ross, A., *Pagan Celtic Britain*, Cardinal, London, 1974

– *Folklore of the Scottish Highlands*, Batsford, London, 1976

– *Life and Death of a Druid Prince*, London, 1989

Smith, M., *The Triads of Britain* (compiled by Iolo Morgannwg), Wildwood Press, 1977

Spence, L., *The Mysteries of Britain*, London, 1939

Tatlock, J. S. P., *The Legendary History of Britain*, Berkeley, 1950

Thorpe, L. (trans.), *The History of the Kings of Britain* (of Geoffrey of Monmouth), Penguin Books, Harmondsworth, 1966

Tolstoy, N., *The Quest for Merlin*, Hamish Hamilton, London, 1985

Williams, Sir Ifor, *Lectures on early Welsh Poetry*, Dublin Institute for Advanced Studies

Wimberley, L., *Folklore in the English and Scottish Ballads*, New York, 1959

Yates, Frances, *The Art of Memory*, London, 1959

Books by Robin Williamson

The Craneskin Bag: Celtic Stories and Poems, Canongate, Edinburgh, 1989

Selected Writings: 1980–83, Pigs Whisker Press, 1984

Selected Books by R. J. Stewart

Advanced Magical Arts, Element Books, Shaftesbury, 1988

Celtic Gods and Goddesses, Blandford Press, London, 1990

Celtic Myths, Celtic Legends, Blandford Press, London, 1994

Cuchulainn, Firebird Books, Poole, 1988

The Dreamerpower Tarot, deck and book by R. J. Stewart, paintings by Stuart Littlejohn, Aquarian Press (HarperCollins), London, 1993

Earthlight, Element Books, Shaftesbury, 1992

Elements of Creation Myth, Element Books, Shaftesbury, 1989

Elements of Prophecy, Element Books, Shaftesbury, 1990

Legendary Britain (with John Matthews), Blandford Press, London, 1989

Living Magical Arts, Blandford Press, Poole/London, 1987

The Living World of Faery, Gothic Image Press, Glastonbury, 1995

Merlin: The Prophetic Vision and the Mystic Life, Penguin Arkana, London, 1994

The Merlin Tarot, Aquarian Press, Wellingborough, 1988. Two-volume book and deck of full colour cards, artwork by Miranda Gray

Power within the Land, Element Books, Shaftesbury, 1993

Robert Kirk, Walker Between Worlds, a new edition of *The Secret Commonwealth* in modern English with commentary, Element Books, Shaftesbury, 1991

The Underworld Initiation, Aquarian Press, Wellingborough, 1984 and 1989

Warriors of Arthur (with John Matthews), Blandford Press, Poole/London, 1987

Where is St George?, Moonraker Press/Humanities Press, USA/Blandford Press, London, 1976, 1978, 1988

INDEX

Page numbers in *italic* refer to illustrations